ST. PIUS V

OTHER WORKS BY THE AUTHOR

Rome Churches for English-Speaking People

The Quiet Grave—Intimate Journals

Between Two Wars—The Life of Pius XI

Gleams of English-Language Literature

Pope Pius VII—His Life, Times, and
Struggle with Napoleon in the
Aftermath of the French Revolution

ST. PIUS V

A Brief Account of His
Life, Times, Virtues and Miracles

By

Robin Anderson

Foreword by

Alfredo Cardinal Ottaviani

TAN BOOKS AND PUBLISHERS, INC.
Rockford, Illinois 61105

Originally published in 1973 by St. Michael's Press. Republished in 1978 by TAN Books and Publishers, Inc. Retypeset and republished again in 1989 by TAN Books and Publishers, Inc. Typography is the property of TAN Books and Publishers, Inc., and may not be reproduced, in whole or in part, without written permission of the publisher.

Library of Congress Catalog Card Number: 88-51510

ISBN: 0-89555-354-6

The photo on the front cover is of the statue of Pope St. Pius V by Leonardo da Sarzana located in the Sistine Chapel of St. Mary Major's Basilica in Rome.

Printed and bound in the United States of America.

TAN BOOKS AND PUBLISHERS, INC.
P.O. Box 424
Rockford, Illinois 61105

1989

PRAYER TO ST. PIUS V
from the Dominican Liturgy

O St. Pius V, admirable Pastor, remember thy flock! Before the Supreme Judge of all, come to the aid of thy faithful! Who can better intercede for us? For none labored more intensely to further God's glory on earth.

CONTENTS

SOME PRINCIPAL DATES
IN THE LIFE OF ST. PIUS V

1504	Birth
1518	Enters Dominican College
1521	Religious Profession
1528	Ordination
1545	Opening of Council of Trent
1546	Appointed Inquisitor at Como
1550	Inquisitor General
1556	Bishop of Nepi and Sutri (under Paul IV)
1557	Created Cardinal with title of S. Maria Sopra Minerva
1558	Inquisitor General of Christendom
1560	Bishop of Mondovi (under Pius IV)
1563	Closing of the Council of Trent
1566	Elected Pope
1566	Catechism of the Council of Trent
1568	The Roman Breviary—*Quod a nobis*
1570	The Roman Missal— *Quo primum tempore*
1570	Excommunication of Elizabeth— *Regnans in excelsis*
1571	Signing of the Triple Holy Alliance against the Turks
1571	The Battle of Lepanto
1572	Death (May 1)
1588	Mortal remains transferred from St. Peter's Basilica to St. Mary Major's
1672	Beatification by Clement X
1712	Canonization by Clement XI
1904	Repositioning and reclothing of the sacred remains

FOREWORD

This book by Prof. Anderson does something truly opportune and praiseworthy in giving an account of the virtues and merits of St. Pius V, great saint, glorious defender of Christian standards, valiant guardian of the treasures of truth, justice and sanctity which the Church was born to spread throughout the world.

And this is all the more opportune in our age when materialism, Communism, humanism and atheism *"convenerunt in unum adversus Dominum et adversus Christum ejus."*

God's mysterious designs were revealed in a singular way when Michael Ghislieri, withdrawn from the particular and limited duties of a local apostolate, was elected to the Throne of the Supreme Pontificate.

Rome, the Church, the entire world needed a man of the temper, holiness and energetic action such as were proper to him.

Mohammedanism threatened a devastating storm, but Providence raised up the man who might be the worthy and fitting instrument to subdue it.

Lepanto gave Christendom no mere passing victory of restricted range and importance; it was the mainspring of the recovery that freed the Christian world from a disastrous reverse and enabled the Church to carry on her evangelizing mission with security.

And in this regard it should indeed be clearly shown how the Supreme Pontificate was then, and always will be, the effective bulwark of salvation.

I wrote once, and wish to repeat today, this indisputable judgment on the mission of papal Rome: "All sorrow, disaster, darkness or persecution are nothing when we have the certainty that among men there is, and will ever be, a man in whom the light of everlasting truth can never fail. The night of the world is dark for us, but never starless: there is the Pope." And such a light was St. Pius V.

Rome, March 21, 1973

✠ A. Card. OTTAVIANI

Chapter 1

FROM SHEPHERD BOY TO POPE

Michael Ghislieri[1] was born in the township of Bosco, not far from the Piedmontese city of Alesandria, on January 17, 1504, during the reign of Pope Julius II. He was at first called Anthony, but later took the name of Michael, Prince of the Heavenly Hosts, whom he chose as patron. His parents were peasants of deeply Christian faith.

As a boy, he had a special love for the Mother of God and wished to consecrate himself to God's service. His mother encouraged him prudently, telling him to pray to Our Lady. When he was twelve years old, this desire became the certainty that he had a vocation to be a priest. His people were too poor, however, to afford him studies and set him to mind the flocks of sheep.

According to some accounts, a chance meeting with two Dominican Fathers in the fields decided his entry into religion: struck by the boy's piety and intelligence, the Friars suggested his studying Latin with them and trying his vocation. There are also contemporary references to a gentleman of the

---

[1] Also spelled Ghisleri, and Ghisilieri.

neighborhood sending him to the Dominicans for schooling, together with his son. His progress was anyway so remarkable that after two years, with his parents' consent, he was allowed to take the habit of the order.

He was professed the following year, then sent to Bologna University, where he obtained the requisite degrees and was appointed professor of philosophy for the province when only twenty years old. As well as having a gift for imparting knowledge, he was able to instill a love of supernatural virtue, more by example than by eloquence. Of his theological teaching it was said he "mingled the thorns of Calvary with those of learning," leading his pupils to the foot of the Cross.

Ordained at twenty-four in 1528, he was to say his first Mass, by the wish of his Provincial, in the parish church of his birthplace. He arrived to find it burnt down, his home half destroyed, and the church desecrated by imperial troops. Rome had been occupied and sacked the previous year, and Pope Clement VII was still the Emperor Charles V's prisoner in Castel St. Angelo. He said his first Mass in Sezze, where his parents had taken refuge.

Four times elected Prior, although he would have refused the responsibility had it been possible to do so without going against the will of God, he never dispensed himself from the least observance of the Rule. Tired out from his teaching work, he practiced additional mortifications to keep himself from becoming vain over the success he had with his students. His government was gentle, but severe;

and the open or veiled dislike aroused in some by his sternness caused him acute suffering. His health was not always good, but his stall was never empty during Divine Office in choir, for which he was punctual to the minute. Never leaving the monastery himself except on necessary business, he would not allow the younger monks to go outside the enclosure. "Salt when thrown into water becomes indistinguishable from it," he said, "and religious, by God's grace the salt of the earth, easily absorb the spirit of the world when unnecessarily in contact with it."

When a band of hungry, marauding soldiers one day appeared at the gates, fiercely threatening pillage and destruction, a few courageous and compassionate words from the holy Prior persuaded the men instead to become his guests in the monastery, where they remained, with good behavior, sharing in the life of the community until circumstances enabled them to depart.

His reputation for sanctity soon spread far beyond the monastery and many put themselves under his spiritual direction, causing him further spiritual and physical suffering. He became Confessor to the Spanish governor of Milan, making the journey to and from the city on foot, in all weathers and in silence only broken for recitation of the Breviary and Rosary with his travelling companion. Urged to buy a thicker cloak for winter weather, he would not, asking what sort of poverty monks professed who went clothed as comfortably as those in the world.

Everywhere at this time there was strife, rebel-

lion and discord. Heresy, open or concealed, was
spreading continually. The Protestant Reformation
had found its way into Northern Italy via Switzerland, which teamed with propagators of the new
doctrines, and many of the Lombard clergy in particular, consciously or unconsciously, had been affected. The Cardinals of the Sacred College advised
severe measures and Pope Paul III in 1542 decided
that the best means would be to reorganize the
Roman Inquisition.[2] At a Provincial Chapter the
following year, the Dominican Fathers called on the
Prior whose fame was known to them to speak concerning the Lutheran heresy and papal authority.
This he did so ably and with such love for the
Church and papacy that when Rome made inquiries
as to the man most suited for the office of Inquisitor in the important Northern outpost of Como,
he was unanimously recommended.

The chief danger was from books being brought
into Italy via Switzerland. As well as being sold
in shops, they were also hawked from one country
town to another where the simple and unsuspecting

---

[2] Tribunal entrusted by Gregory IX in 1233 to the Dominicans with the duty of searching out heretics, trying them and
delivering them, if guilty and unrepentant, to the secular power
which treated heresy as a crime worse than murder for attacking the life of the soul.

The Roman Inquisition is to be distinguished from the Spanish Inquisition, half civil, half ecclesiastical, authorized in the
15th century to deal with apostasy to Mohammedanism and
Judaism. The Spanish Inquisition was liable to become an instrument of the State; but abuses were much exaggerated by
anti-Catholic propagandists.

townsfolk were often taken in by the contents, cleverly disguised, but against Catholic doctrine, faith and morals. The Inquisitor had to be constantly travelling up and down in order to exercise due vigilance and prevent this activity.

One bookseller, who had been warned, went on disposing of his wares in secret. When discovered, and on having the books confiscated, he appealed to the Vicar Capitular who was administering the vacant diocese. The latter, from jealousy or resentment of the authority exercised by Rome's envoy, persuaded the Canons to stand by the rights of the bookseller. The Inquisitor's prompt excommunication of the Vicar Capitular stirred up such hostility on all sides that he was obliged to return to Rome, where his drastic and timely action was fully upheld.

Sent on a mission to Bergamo, where Lutheranism had been gaining headway with many of the clergy, he was advised to put off his religious habit, lest it endanger him. He declined, saying he had accepted death in undertaking the mission and could not wish to die in a better cause. One of the city's lawyers, wealthy and eminent, whom none had dared oppose, was rash enough to sing the praises of Protestants in the presence of the Inquisitor, further claiming that it was harmful for the common good to fight the new doctrines now widely admitted. The Inquisitor had the lawyer arrested, then faced a group of dumbfounded and furious townsfolk with such a calm and determined defense of his action that he won them over—all but one person, to whose ears the matter had come: the Bishop of the diocese, who sided with the lawyer. The Inquisitor had orders to watch the Bishop, who was known to be surrounded by heretics; but the latter, not liking this vigilance, sent an armed force by night to the monastery where the Inquisitor was lodging. Once again, he contrived to escape and returned to Rome.

Here he had scant welcome this time from the Dominican monastery of Santa Sabina. It was Christmas Eve, he was wet and cold; but on asking for shelter, and fodder for his mule, he was stiffly reminded that the Rule forbade a friar to come to Rome without permission.

But he was made welcome and supported at the Vatican, although a Prelate there remarked he had perhaps been too severe. "Nothing can be too severe," was the undaunted Inquisitor's reply, "for those who attempt to hinder the ministers of religion in their rightful duties by means of the civil power."

Proceedings were instituted against the Bishop, who was deposed and exiled.

In 1550 Pope Julius III appointed him General Commissary of the Roman Inquisition, or Holy Office, and in the performance of his new duties he proved the falseness of the accusation that he was more bent on punishing than converting. On his daily visitations to the detained he did all he could to clear up doubts and dispel error. His kindness, and help given when needed, caused many a change of heart, repentance and conversion.

The best known of his penitents was Sixtus of Siena, a young Jew who had become a Catholic, and a Franciscan. A brilliant preacher, he was in time discovered to hold heretical views on free will and predestination, which he clung to, claiming they threw light on much that was obscure in the Catholic religion! Struck by the personality of the young religious, and pitying his dejection, the Inquisitor won his confidence, offered Masses for him and succeeded in leading him back to the Faith. He finally begged the Pope for his release, and Sixtus was allowed to enter religion again as a Dominican, later becoming one of the greatest Scripture scholars of the period.

Cardinal Caraffa became Pope Paul IV in 1555 and not only confirmed Michael Ghislieri in office as Commissary General of the Inquisition, but also made him Bishop of Nepi and Sutri, diocese near Rome. Then he was made Cardinal, with the altogether exceptional dignity of General Inquisitor of all Christendom, having jurisdiction over all other Inquisitors.

Cardinal Alessandrino (as he was now known, the name given to him from Alessandria, the nearest city to his birthplace) never changed his former simple way of life, which continued to be that of a Dominican monk, and he still wore his rough white habit.[3]

Relentless as was the war he waged against heresy, he nevertheless sought to dissuade the authorities from taking too rigorous action. This, and his defense of the Archbishop of Toledo, imprisoned by

---

[3] It is thought that the popes' wearing white originated thus with St. Pius V.

the Spanish Inquisition for suspected heresy, earned him a rebuff from the Pope who, though his friend, on one occasion called him a "de-friared friar, a Lutheran," and during a Consistory kept him standing for half an hour before the other Cardinals whilst he inveighed against him, declaring that he almost regretted having made him a Cardinal and that he was not worthy of the Purple.

In 1559 Paul IV was succeeded by Pius IV, of very different character, and far less strict. The final stage of the Council of Trent was concluded under him and he continued to make use of the Inquisition; but he was easygoing in regard to heresy. He too confirmed Cardinal Alessandrino in office; but by appointing him Bishop of the distant diocese of Mondovi he virtually exiled from Rome one who had been among Paul IV's chief counsellors and almost the only Cardinal of strong and resolute character.

Hardly had the new Bishop had time to set about the much-needed reform of his new diocese than he was summoned back to Rome, largely at the insistence of Cardinal Borromeo, Archbishop of Milan, who had made his uncle the Pope realize the desirability of having the Inquisitor General near him. His counsels, too, were indispensable in bringing the Council of Trent to a close.

* * *

Urged by the protests of long-suffering French Catholics, and by the proofs brought forward by the Inquisitor General, Pius IV advised the Cardinals of the Inquisition to proceed against a number of

French Bishops accused of betraying their teaching office and favoring the Protestants. Cardinal Alessandrino summoned the Bishops to acquit themselves in Rome of the charges against them. The Regent of France, Catherine de Medici, making a political question out of a purely religious one, declared that the rights of the Crown and freedom of the Gallican Church were at stake; then sent an ambassador to the Pope. When this ambassador proved to be none other than one of the indicted Bishops, Cardinal Alessandrino prevailed upon Pius IV not to receive him until he had either retracted or established his innocence. The other French Bishops next failing to present themselves, Cardinal Alesandrino advocated certain of them being declared heretics and deprived of office, others being forbidden to govern their dioceses unless admitting their errors. He did this so ably that, although not all the Cardinals agreed, the Pope approved the proposed sentences, which he could hardly not have done without causing serious scandal.

Cardinal Alessandrino had often to speak to the Pontiff with extreme firmness, although by so doing he risked losing favor and confidence. He was the only adviser who dared try and dissuade Pius IV (but without success) from making two young princes Cardinals, one of them a boy of thirteen. But when it came to disagreeing with the Sovereign Pontiff over having his favorite nephew paid several thousand ducats out of the papal treasury he did finally fall into disgrace and might have been confined in Castel St. Angelo had not Cardinal

Borromeo again spoken on his behalf.

He now suffered so much from hostile intrigue and the curtailment of his powers that, although serenely aware of having only done his duty, he thought of returning to Mondovi. But it seems certain members of the Sacred College urged the Pope not to let the Inquisitor General go. He himself, on hearing that the ship carrying his baggage had been captured by pirates, and at the same time becoming seriously indisposed, asked the Pope's leave to remain in Rome.

Then, whilst Cardinal Alessandrino was recovering from the first attack of the complaint that was to bring about his death in a few years, Pius IV fell ill and died.

There was no more need for him to leave Rome; nor, by God's providence, did he ever do so again.

* * *

After some attempts had been made at the ensuing Conclave to elect a successor by majority vote, Cardinal Farnese was induced by Cardinal Borromeo, who had most influence in the Sacred College, to renounce his aspiration to the papacy and join him and the others in choosing Cardinal Alessandrino, whose outstanding virtues and capability were acknowledged by all. Despite the hesitation of some, who may have feared lest the Inquisitor General, if elected, might deal hardly with those of the late Pope's entourage who had opposed him, Cardinal Borromeo, as though guided by God, led his colleagues to Cardinal Alessandrino's cell.

Realizing their intention, he at once intimated his refusal.

But again, as by divine inspiration, this time of one accord, almost by force and against his own will, the Cardinals led him into the Pauline Chapel.

There, after a noisy discussion as to the mode of election, they decided that, one by one, each should declare himself in favor of Cardinal Alessandrino; and, beginning with the Cardinal Dean, this was done.

All then rising and acclaiming the newly elected, he was asked by the Cardinal Dean whether he accepted.

The answer was silence.

On the Cardinals' insisting, the words at length came from him: *"Mi contento sù,"* signifying consent.

So, by an altogether unexpected turn of events, the Conclave that had dragged on for over three weeks was brought to an end in a matter of less than three hours.

It would have been natural for the new Pope to take the name of Paul, after his friend and protector Paul IV; but out of regard for Cardinal Borromeo he took the name of the latter's uncle, Pius—the first characteristic act of self-abnegation on the part of the newly-elected pontiff.

There was great rejoicing among the Cardinals, and in the Eternal City, in the knowledge that the world had been given a Sovereign Pontiff of such great holiness of life and firmness of character, sorely needed by the times.

Chapter 2

SOVEREIGN PONTIFF AND
TEMPORAL REFORM

When in 1566 Cardinal Alessandrino became Pope Pius V he was sixty-two years old. Informed of certain of the Roman people's surprise and disappointment at his election—perhaps some feared his penances might now be imposed upon themselves, or that he had too little experience of government and the world to hold the reins—Pius is said to have remarked that if joy had been lacking at his election, he hoped there would be regret at his death.

But if at first some of the Romans feared the new Pope's austerities, his action at the outset of his reign made them soon realize how much, by this very life of prayer and self-denial, his great love of God overflowed in works of utmost benefit to others.

Rumors that his health would not let him reign for more than a few months were contradicted by his evident vigor. He himself declared that he felt better as Pope than he had as Cardinal. A report of the Florentine ambassador, among others, referred to the reigning Pontiff as "flourishing like a rose."

The gloomy mood of some of the populace had already begun to change on the day of his coronation, and crowds turned out in big festivity with acclamations of "Long live Pius V!" At Pius IV's coronation, persons had been trodden under foot in the scramble for the coins customarily thrown by the Pope on this occasion to the people. Pius V abolished this, distributing instead sums of money to the needy in their homes and also to the poorer monasteries and convents.

His first act after being crowned was to dismiss the papal court jester, and no pope has had one since.

At the banquet that followed, he ate as little as though he had been in a monastery refectory. The next year the anniversary banquet was done away with and the money that would have been spent on it given to good works.

The Roman people began to love him as a father, the more they realized his goodness and holiness; and on his public appearances he was greeted with a jubilation not known in ten previous pontificates.

The profound impression made by the white-robed Dominican Friar, once a shepherd, now Supreme Pastor of the Universal Church, was noted in report after report of the ambassadors in Rome. The Spanish ambassador affirmed that for three hundred years the Church had not had a better head, adding: "This Pope is a saint."

As temporal sovereign of Rome, Pius V set out to bring greater order, health and beauty to the Eternal City. Among his first acts were the repairing of sacred buildings, of aqueducts and walls, the renewing of fortifications, and the opening of workshops and factories to provide employment and keep the people from idleness and vice. Schools were set up in which parents could get good free education for their children.

Provision was made for beggars, who were allotted special quarters, and priests were assigned to instruct them in Christian living and give them the Sacraments.

Merchants and dealers were forbidden to use the images of saints as trademarks and shop signs.

To keep holy Sundays and Feastdays, measures were taken against the custom of playing games on these days.

Gazettes and periodicals were prevented from spreading scandalous and calumnious reports.

The papal treasury was drained on behalf of the poor, the Pope himself living on a bare minimum, even in penury—his table was known to be the poorest of any.

When plague broke out after famine he organized a relief committee for the distribution of food, clothing, medicine and funds, going himself on foot to bring comfort and help to the suffering and dying. He provided and paid for a staff of priests and doctors to attend the sick, administer the Sacraments and bury the dead.[1]

---

[1] A constitution obliging doctors to exhort patients to receive the Sacrament of Penance, and to suspend visits unless written testimony were forthcoming of compliance or valid reasons for non-compliance, had no general application. Although it was based on an injunction of the IV Lateran Council, theologians and canonists differed as to binding circumstances and the extent to which doctors should hold themselves bound.

Jail regulations were reformed and imprisonment for debt forbidden.

Pius V was tireless in ransoming Christian slaves from the Turks, housing and clothing them at his own expense.

His charity to English Catholics exiled for their religion was boundless.

A Constitution supporting and protecting agricultural labor was successfully applied, and became justly famed. Pius V took steps to prevent further pollution of the Tiber, at the same time assuring Rome the best supply of drinking water brought from the Salone to the Trevi fountains.

In all these works the Pope's right-hand was his nephew Cardinal Bonelli, also a Dominican. He had made his relative a member of the Sacred College and given him this responsibility only when his belief had been shaken in the disinterestedness of Cardinal Farnese and others, some of whom depended on temporal princes and minded more their own than the Church's interests. The young Cardinal Bonelli, chosen for his trustworthiness, ability and austere character, though only 25, was not allowed to hold any benefices, make gifts to relatives or receive any; and he was strictly enjoined to be true to his religious vocation by continuing, as Cardinal, to live a life of holy poverty.

When it was suggested to Pius V, who had a horror of nepotism, that he give preference to other relatives, he replied that God had called him to serve the Church, not have the Church serve him.

This firmness toward the members of his own

family still further increased the Roman people's
respect for the new Pope whose government they
saw to be scrupulously fair in everything. Pius' lofty
vision of the papal office, his awareness of never
having had ulterior aims, strengthened the exercise
of his authority and gave him great independence
in governing. Even in temporal administration,
though assisted by Cardinal Bonelli, and later by
others when the work grew overwhelming, it was
evident that the real direction of affairs was kept
firmly in the Pope's hands.[2]

Many of the Cardinals living in luxury justified
this, saying that it was necessary for the prestige
of the Holy See. First putting his own house in
order, Pius did not hesitate to urge them also to
a life of simplicity, even of holy poverty, which he
could safely do, himself setting the example.

Magistrates and civil governors were effectively
exhorted to administer true justice and equity without delay. When possible, Pius personally super-
vised their appointment. Bad governors were severely
taken to task and punished—one, for crimes including rape, was beheaded. A weekly public congregation was started at which any might voice
complaints as to justice being postponed or mal-
administered.

Pius V not only made laws for the improvement
of public morality, he also saw that these laws were

---

[2] Toward the end of his reign, Pius V expressed his intention
of withdrawing altogether from temporal concerns so as to
attend solely to the Inquisition.

put into force and so successfully that, within a year, the change that came over Rome was manifest. Pilgrims and visitors noticed it: one foreign witness leaving it on record that "The shaming of Satan and all his ministers by general works of penance and piety is not astonishing under such a pontiff, with his fasts, his humility, innocence, holiness and zeal for the Faith shining so brightly: and if Calvin himself had been able to see him blessing his kneeling people he would, in spite of himself, have recognized and venerated the true representative of Christ."

One of the first blows Pius V dealt to vice and corruption in Rome was to banish men and women of light morals from the city. Those underestimating the Pope's resoluteness by appealing for such a surprising and drastic measure to be revoked were told that, on the contrary, rather than so much as appear to allow licentiousness of any kind in the holy city and capital of Christendom, he would transfer his court elsewhere.

Courtisans and prostitutes were given as alternative to banishment marriage or being put to live in a penitential institute. Some, accepting banishment, were killed by highwaymen. A number voluntarily reformed their lives and returned to the practice of their religion. But so deep-rooted was the evil that Pius had to counter it all through his reign. He had this reform much at heart and later persuaded a group of virtuous women to devote themselves wholly to the difficult work. Generous aid of every kind was provided for those converted to a better way of living.

Grieved and indignant over the prevalence of adultery in Rome, Pius V could hardly be prevented from instituting the death penalty for it; but he had culprits publicly punished irrespective of their position: A nobleman was sentenced to life imprisonment, a well-known banker to flogging.

The penalty for sodomy was burning.

Disreputable taverns were closed, despite the plea that this was bad for business. To all criticism of such kind Pius replied that the good of souls must come before considerations of revenue.

On the other hand, he allowed and encouraged innocent games and amusements, but forbade horse-racing in St. Peter's Square.

Towards evil-doers Pius V was inexorable, insisting on sentences once passed being carried out. In his efforts to restore the good name of Paul IV, whose statue had been knocked down and rolled into the Tiber by some of the people, he resorted to capital punishment for those guilty of having willfully maligned the Pope and his memory.

In his fight against lawlessness and banditry, the nobility of Pius' character was well shown when, all attempts at capturing a notorious brigand having failed, one of the man's relatives offered to decoy him by inviting him to a meal in his house. Pope Pius would not hear of so base and treacherous a means. On being told of this, the bandit left papal territory of his own free will.

But it was not only brigands that Pius V had trouble from; he also had to contend with factious nobles whose ranks were swelled by outlaws, exiles, runaway soldiers and even rebel monks in conflict with his disciplinary and reforming measures. These were sometimes joined by heretics or Catholics with heretical sympathies.

Learning that the city of Faenza was riddled with factions and heresy, Pius wanted to demolish it and have the inhabitants transferred elsewhere—but he had to be content with less drastic action.

His strenuous efforts were on the whole successful. There was greater quiet throughout the pontifical States during his reign, and the good effects of his legislation were generally acknowledged. Some reports of the time refer to Pope Pius' severe chastisement of vices sometimes including minor offenses, but instances are not specified.

Pius V's bold and energetic exercise of his authority was noted in the report of the Venetian ambassador the year after he came to the throne. Counsellors warned the Pope to pay heed to what he was about for fear of provoking the few practicing Catholics that remained into defying or shunning his authority. But Pius did not change, taking little counsel from Cardinals or anyone else, knowing that in Rome more than in other places people are inclined to speak and act in order to please another, or flatter the Pope, but in all ways to procure their own advantage. He had ever found that what he undertook ended well, Pius said, because it was directed to the good and so favored by God.

The Venetian ambassador's report did hint at the new Pope's liability to form hasty judgments, but without detailing any; and after declaring that his qualities were hard to believe compared with those of previous pontiffs, the report relates how Pius V confided that he wanted sovereigns "to draw all things from the Spirit rather than from the temporal," being of the opinion his authority extended over all States and that he could absolutely command in everything.[3] In this regard the Pope quoted St. Thomas Aquinas, saying that Constantine did not give to the Church but *rendered to her what was hers,* thereby inferring that there is nothing in the world that is not of the Church.

Unqualified praise is found in a discerning paragraph of the already quoted Spanish ambassador: "Rarely indeed in a pope has the monarch so given place to the priest: one thing only he has at heart, the salvation of souls. This is what determines his entire policy; on this he bases every service and reckons the value of every institution and act."

As Inquisitor General, Pius V had been familiar with the affected righteousness concerning religious art of the Protestant reformers, who were in reality destroyers of true culture and beauty, and of the way they justified their attitude by pointing to the lack of pure Christian inspiration in contemporary sacred art. Pius did not conceal his aversion for

---

[3] The Bull *In Coena Domini* (of uncertain date) affirming a measure of suzerainty for the Holy See over temporal sovereigns, was given legal force by Pope Julius II, and Pius V confirmed this. But the Emperor, and some princes, refused to accept clauses concerning ecclesiastical jurisdiction and property; and from then on the Bull's decrees were dropped.

the licentious spirit of much Renaissance "humanistic" art. But, not unlike some of the Renaissance popes before him, he neither condemned nor held himself aloof from contemporary art but set about seeing that it should be used in the service of truth and religion. Aided by Cardinal Borromeo and Philip Neri, he engaged the best artists—Vasari, Vignola, Zuccari, Della Porta—to apply their new and more perfect techniques of perspective to religious subjects, often directly suggested by him, so as to enshrine in painting, as well as in sculpture and architecture, the radiant ideals of the Catholic religion.

The building of the new St. Peter's went ahead under Pius V, who was much preoccupied over the question of vaulting the cupola. In 1567 Vasari was called to Rome for consultation, and it was agreed not to deviate by a hair's breadth from the original design of Michaelangelo, Vasari taking credit for influencing the Pope in the matter.

It was also by order of Pius V that work was begun on the church of St. Mary of the Angels built above the chapel in the Umbrian plain where St. Francis of Assisi died.

The better to direct people's minds to concepts of religion, Pope Pius further replaced the mythological tags formerly in vogue on pontifical medals by inscriptions such as *Hodie in terra canunt angeli* —This day do the angels sing on earth; *Impera Domine et fac tranquillitatem*—O Lord, speak the word and there will be peace; and *Dextera Domini fecit virtutem*—The right hand of the Lord has struck with power; and not since the time of Cimabue and Giotto, it was judged, had frescoes and paintings better reflected the Christian spirit.[4]

Pius V's measures, as temporal sovereign of Rome, in regard to the Jews need to be judged according to the situation of the times. In its dealings with necromancy, divination and witchcraft connected with the Renaissance "humanistic" movement, the Inquisition had frequently to do with Jews. This was nothing new since Juvenal Iunius and others were writing in the first centuries of Christianity about such activity on the part of Jews in Rome. Time and again expelled from various Italian States for these and other activities undermining Christian society they had, within limits, been tolerated by the Popes. Some, taking advantage of this, had grown rich on usury, bringing whole families to want and corruption; others, setting themselves up as doctors, were in fact engaged in profitable drug traffic, the magic arts and fortune-telling, trading on the superstitious beliefs of ignorant people.

Whilst dealing strictly with the Jews at the beginning of his reign, Pius at the same time made it a punishable offense to insult them. But the offenses committed by Jews, some of whom showed

---

[4] Pius V did propose that the Vatican Belvedere statuary be removed and donated to the Roman people, on the grounds that "pagan effigies" did not suitably adorn the domains of Peter's Successor. But yielding to the remonstrances of some Cardinals, he ordered the statues to be preserved in an enclosed collection and kept by the director of the Vatican botanical gardens (which he had created).

hatred for Christianity by putting themselves in the service of Turks and infidels, sworn enemies of Christ, obliged the Pope at length to issue an edict banishing them from the Papal States, whilst granting them certain territory in Rome, and in the northern city of Ancona.

How greatly Pius V had the true well-being and conversion of the Jews at heart was shown by his having special preaching courses organized for them. He himself baptized those who became Christians and provided for their care under Jesuit spiritual direction. When the seventy-year-old synagogue president became a Christian, together with his three sons, he was baptized by the Pope with great solemnity in St. Peter's, many Cardinals and crowds of people attending. Others followed the chief Rabbi's example, moved, as they declared, by the great piety, bounty and holiness they saw in the life and actions of the Pope.

Pius V's day began with Mass said very early, preceded by a long meditation and followed by an equally long thanksgiving. He said the Rosary daily; and he had a special devotion to prayer for the dead, to which he attached several indulgences, and to St. Michael, his patron.

He often spent hours a day, sometimes from sunrise until afternoon scarcely pausing to take a little nourishment, hearing the complaints of the people, giving preference to the poorest.

Out of love for the Blessed Sacrament, he would never allow himself to be carried at the *Corpus Christi* procession, but went on foot bearing the

Monstrance. His expression, recollection and humble bearing on these occasions were enough to make people return to the practice of their Faith.

During the Roman carnival, which he did not forbid, though it was forbidden for men to dress up as women, and vice-versa, or in religious costume, the Pope would be seen daily walking through the city, saying the Rosary, paying no heed to the masked figures in fancy dress with whom at times he almost rubbed shoulders.

Crowds would gather to see him pass or watch him enter a church or basilica. Some English apostates who had gathered by the way, together with a band of Protestants, to mock publicly at Catholicism, were so struck by the Pope's demeanor and manifest supernatural faith that they admitted their error and again professed their former religious belief.

Though often short of funds, but not lacking advisers pressing him to accept substantial sums in view of dispensations (as had been customary with some popes before him), Pius V steadfastly refused to do so, thereby greatly enhancing his authority and increasing the people's respect for the papacy.

He remarked to a well-meaning Bishop who laid before him a scheme for improving the Church's finances that Christianity could get along well enough with prayer and exemplary life, and had no need of treasure. When hard-pressed for money to finance projects such as helping the Catholics of France in their struggle against the Huguenots he was, however, reluctantly compelled to levy taxes, but chiefly on the rich, the well-off clergy included.

These things being generally known to the people, disorders gradually grew less and were replaced by honesty, good manners and sincerity.

Despite his own rigid economy, rather, on account of it, Pope Pius managed to be unfailingly bountiful towards impoverished members of the clergy as well as needy employees deserving of assistance.

His efforts for the furthering of true learning did not stop at setting up schools for the people, but were especially concentrated on the Roman university. He not only saw that work on the new buildings was duly carried on but, by getting rid of administrative abuses, he also straightened out its tottering finances.

It is strange, then, after this, to find the great papal historian von Pastor, who has nothing but praise for Pius V's spiritual reforms and Church government, writing that he was not happy in all his projects as temporal sovereign. The imputation, if such it be, of a certain lack of practical and administrative capacity (inconsistent with highest sanctity) is borne out by very few instances of any great importance, one a matter of coinage issue.

In times of dearth, monopoly and profiteering were efficaciously prohibited by Pope Pius and special watch was kept over provisions and stores so that all could at least buy bread at a good price, having in mind the saying: *"Qui abscondit frumenta, maledicitur in populis"*—He that hides up grain shall be cursed among the people. (*Prov.* 2:26).

"All Rome gloried in its holy Pastor," wrote again

the Venetian ambassador, "and the people have so much faith in him that when plague broke out they turned to him with prayers asking his intercession with God to avert the scourge..."

In recognition of his very great services to the city, the Roman Senate wanted to put up a statue of him. But Pius would not permit it.

Symbolic of the motive in all he undertook and accomplished was his altering of the Rome University motto: *"Quod bonum faustum felixque sit"*— May what is good be lucky and happy—to: *"In nomine Sanctissimae atque individuae Trinitatis"*—In the name of the Most Holy and Undivided Trinity; and what better witness and monument to all his work of temporal renewal could there have been than the manifest change that in a short time came over the face of Rome, so as to make it once more seen and called a Holy City.

Chapter 3

SPIRITUAL REFORM

The deplorable state in which Pius V found the Church on his becoming Pope made him apply himself with the utmost unremitting energy to getting rid of abuses and corruption. He had to deal with an inherited situation that might have seemed ruinous but for Christ's promise that the gates of Hell will never prevail. Repeated yieldings and compromises on every front had allowed Protestantism to spread, with its negation of the supernatural, of the priesthood and the Sacraments; and it appeared to triumph in more and more places, affording proof that it was not so much authoritarianism as laxism that, by refusing to issue clear commands and set fixed limits, engendered false creeds, individual rebellion, and contestation.

Not only had feeble resistance to the innovators been offered by Emperor and Catholic sovereigns, but also, in spite of Trent, false hopes had continued to be entertained—it seems even by Pius V's very predecessor—of winning Protestants by making concessions to them regarding the rite of Communion, and ecclesiastical discipline.

The guiding principle in all that Pius V undertook

was the exact and rigorous application of the decrees of the Council of Trent; and it was thanks to his determined energy that these decrees did not remain a dead letter, as those of some previous Councils, such as Constance and the V Lateran. The magnitude of Pius V's achievement is moreover measured by the fact of his reforms having been successfully applied not only in Italy and Europe, but throughout the Catholic world then being expanded by the discovery of new continents.

On becoming Pope, Pius V had not only continued wearing the Dominican habit, he had preserved the grace of his state of religious perfection, of which the habit is an outward sign and distinction. His spirit of faith and prayer, simplicity of outlook, uprightness and loyalty enabled him to avoid contamination and complicity with the spirit and powers of the world, with which the devil tempted Christ Himself in the wilderness. Pope Pius' spiritual reform started with the members of his own household. A model of virtue and penance himself, he gave them a rule of life, constantly exhorting them to shun ambition and vice, to cultivate virtue. He openly told them he would not tolerate any in his court who did not live according to Christian precepts and standards. A priest famed for his sanctity was further called to take charge of the moral reform of the papal court, which would have repercussions on the Cardinals and Curia, thence on Rome and Christendom.

The Pope told the Cardinals in his first allocution that he wished to have dealings with them as brothers, and that it scarcely behooved their dignity to seek audience with him ten at a time, as had been the custom, but they should come to him one by one and he was willing to receive them at all hours. He reminded the Cardinals that not least among the causes of the spreading of heresy was the lax and unedifying life led by many of the clergy and urged them all to do penance, avoid luxury and reform their style of living. Those that complied received the Pope's special confidence and favor.

Pius V refused a request of the imperial envoy in Rome for the Red Hat to be conferred on a certain prelate, saying the Church's Senate had already been too much increased in numbers, to the detriment of its prestige and quality. The Cardinals he did create were chosen for their merit and attitude, regardless of political or national considerations.

Some of the Pope's former confreres in religion who began to appear frequently at the Vatican were told they ought to stay in their monasteries and that they would be sent for if needed. The same independence was shown by Pius towards the Jesuits and other orders, from whom he wished to remain free of undue influence.

His first and chief care, after that of his own household, was for the reform of the clergy, since "It is an established fact," he wrote to one Bishop, "that bad priests are the ruin of the people and that odious heresy, introduced by force, has no other aim than that of corrupting the faithful."

For some time past various abuses had been deplored but never remedied. They had even been looked on with indulgence. These Pius V at once set about correcting. Absentee Bishops were ordered to return to their dioceses and govern their flocks as true Pastors and Fathers, within a given time-limit, or be deprived and substituted. All Bishops were urged to make regular canonical visitations and resolutely extirpate evils by enforcing application of existing Church canons, punishing any who would not submit or who tried to withdraw themselves from their jurisdiction on one pretext or another. Finally, Bishops were strongly exhorted to fast and pray, to lead their people by penitential example, and to fight heresy courageously.

Some who withstood the Pope had reason to regret it; and the Archbishop of Cologne, for one, who did so was obliged to resign. Old age, even infirmity, were never accepted by Pius V as reasons for retirement. To the aged Archbishop of Goa who begged to be relieved of the government of his diocese on this account Pius wrote that, like a good soldier, he ought to remain at his post and die on the field of battle if necessary. A touching confidence was added, the Pope acknowledging that he himself, at times, felt a longing to return to the life of a simple religious, but that he had made a resolution never to try and shake off his present yoke.

Pius V was equally energetic in defending the rights and reputation of Bishops, as when a certain prelate of known sanctity was accused of misuse of authority by a member of the Dominican order. Looking into the case personally, and finding the accusation groundless, he had the culprit arrested and punished.

In all, 314 Bishops were elected by Pius V. He chose them all with the greatest care, without yielding to pressure from sovereigns and regardless of worldly interests, for their maturity, sound doctrine, and irreproachable conduct; and he kept in touch with them by correspondence afterwards, without neglecting others.

For all his great humility, gentleness and kindness—indeed, because of his supernatural charity—Pope Pius did not flinch from sternly commanding with the full power of his unique authority, when called for: in restoring the priestly ministry and discipline, in bringing God's ministers back to the essentials and dignity of their sublime vocation. He not only warned them against having any part in temporal affairs that could endanger their spiritual well-being, but absolutely forbade them to accept any employment whatever, except in the service of Cardinals and Catholic princes. Attendance at all kinds of shows and games was forbidden.

Simony was interdicted on pain of excommunication, loss of benefice, even corporal punishment and it was not allowed to cede benefices to relatives either by contract or inheritance. The objection that ecclesiastical revenues would thereby be diminished was met by Pius' answer that poverty was preferable to abuses and Church patrimony could never depend on greed or ambition.

The widespread evil of *commendam*—laymen, sometimes women, paying a priest a salary for performing clerical duties whilst themselves enjoying the revenues—quickly vanished under the stern disciplinary measures of Pope Pius.

Strict regulations were laid down in regard to religious houses and recital of the Divine Office everywhere rendered obligatory. In the first year of his pontificate, in addition to the strong measures adopted against immorality and corruption, Pius V issued an edict laying down the most drastic penalties for disturbance of divine worship, profanation of Sundays and Feastdays, and blasphemy. Strolling, chatting and whispering in church were forbidden, as offending God in the Blessed Sacrament present on the altar and punished by fines or—incredible as it may seem now—by imprisonment and exile. The clergy, with the help of sacristans and other appointed officials, had to see that these regulations were observed.

The parish priests of Rome were ordered to have parents send their children to Sunday school for instruction in Catholic doctrine, as laid down by the Council of Trent, and severely sanctioned if failing to do so.

A special Congregation for the reform of the Index and Correction of Books was created by Pius V, whose experience as Inquisitor had gained him particular knowledge of the untold harm done by bad books. This Congregation had universal jurisdiction, examining pernicious publications and condemning and proscribing them if judged necessary.[1]

Hundreds of Bulls show with what vigor and precision Pius V unflaggingly watched over and defended the deposit of faith, legislating for the safeguarding of doctrine and morals.

The Apostolic Penitentiary was reorganized by Pius V, and he issued decrees reforming various Curia Offices, the Chancery and Datary, as well as the archives.

Abolition of priestly celibacy was advocated by the Emperor Maximilian as a solution for the dearth of vocations, and this solution was supported by certain of the Cardinals. Against this, Pius V unequivocally reaffirmed celibacy and at the same time the obligation of wearing clerical dress and the religious habit—for then, as now, attempts were being made in various ways to make the clergy lose their outwardly recognizable characteristics. Further measures were taken by Pope Pius to procure better discipline, and sanctity, among priests.

Ecclesiastical seminaries were not thought of until the Council of Trent ordered the setting up in every diocese of special training colleges for the formation of future priests; and one positive result of the Elizabethan persecution in England was the founding of such institutes on the continent. Douai College was established by William Allen in France in the second year of Pius V's reign, 1568. The Pope pledged himself most particularly to the carrying

---

[1] Paul IV commissioned the Inquisition to prepare the first general index of forbidden books. Previous to this, catalogues had been published, by private enterprise, for the guidance of the faithful. A Tridentine Index was published by with the approval of Pius IV.

out of the Tridentine decrees in this respect, and many were the Letters he addressed to Bishops calling on them to found seminaries for the defense of vocations and the improvement of priests in virtue and learning.

In the midst of his manifold spiritual reforms, Pius V constantly turned his attention to the foreign missions, sending religious of various orders to different parts of the world, especially to the vast, newly-discovered territories of North and South America, Africa, Asia and India. He set up a Cardinals' Commission to direct a Congregation for the Missions (precursor of *Propaganda Fide*) making it dependent on the Holy See rather than on local sovereigns. With an outlook ahead of the times the Pope wisely instructed the missionaries, in their work of bringing the Gospel to native peoples, to seek also to better their standards of living, get rid of slavery, build dwellings, schools and hospitals. Baptism was not to be given without adequate instruction. Pius V encouraged missionary initiatives for the organizing of native communities apart from the whites as a means of deterring the latter from abuse of power. He insisted much on the missionaries making common endeavors to educate the people in self-government and to aim at training up a native clergy.

In Peru, Venezuela, Mexico, Colombia, Goa and other lands Pius V sowed the good seed of which others after him were to reap the harvests.

Sixty Apostolic Constitutions and Bulls were directed at eradicating abuses and bringing religious orders back to the spirit of their founders and primitive observance, in particular the so-called "mendicant" ones, on whom he conferred special privileges. Some of these, though, were none too pleased with the Pope's attentions when they found he had studied their Rule, had it revised and rid of what he judged superfluities and irregularities. Orders differing too little in scope and character he fused into single congregations. Convinced that heresy had in so many places taken hold on account of decadence, bad example and lax customs, and that the remedy chiefly lay in a return to discipline and strict observance, he dissolved orders that had sunk so low as to be past reforming, paying no heed to worldly interests involved.

One abuse, it seems, he was unsuccessful in trying to get rid of: that of female cooks being employed in some monasteries, on the grounds that men could not be found and if employed from outside were too expensive.

Cardinal Borromeo was charged with the task of suppressing a sort of Third Order known as the *Humiliati* which, from promising beginnings, had grown rich and lax trading in wool. Pretending to submit, some of the members organized armed resistance and tried to shoot the Cardinal whilst he was singing Vespers in his private chapel. Despite Cardinal Borromeo's plea for mercy, his would-be assassins were condemned to death, and after further investigation of the order Pope Pius had a Bull of suppression drawn up and put into effect.

A culminating act of Pius V's spiritual reforms

was his declaring St. Thomas Aquinas a Doctor of the Church. He had a standard edition of the Saint's complete works brought out at his own expense from Vatican manuscripts. This not only served to arouse deeper and more universal knowledge of St. Thomas, but also to counteract current doctrinal deviations and false theologies. The Pope, moreover, followed up his action by making the *Summa Theologica* obligatory teaching in the universities.

Accusations of unduly favoring his own Dominican order could hardly be made with fairness as the Franciscans had also reason for gratitude, the divisive tendencies among their several branches being largely dispelled by the Pope's counsel. Nor did the Jesuits find they need fear his aloofness or disfavor, in spite of recent opposition on the part of some of them to the Dominicans. It did take the Jesuit Superior General some time, however, to submit to the Pope over his commanding the Society of Jesus to recite the Divine Office in choir along with other religious orders, a task St. Ignatius had wished to exempt his sons from; but loyally submit he did in the end.

"I do not deny," Cardinal Newman wrote, "that St. Pius V was stern and severe, as far as a heart burning and melted with divine love could be so. . .Yet such energy and vigor as his were necessary for the times. He was a soldier of Christ in a time of insurrection and rebellion, when, in a spiritual sense, martial law was proclaimed." Such an appraisal the Jesuit General himself, one feels, would have appreciated and endorsed; for Pius V's sternness and severity were first and principally exercised upon *himself* and secondly, in regard to others, only insofar as he believed was for the greater glory of God and His Church. Nor have Church historians been for the most part in doubt that the great impulse everywhere given to faith, morals and piety was owing to him. Few periods in history show a greater number of saints. *Exempla trahunt*—it is example that counts: in St. Pius V, as one of his more recent biographers, Cardinal Grente, has beautifully said, the Catholic Church had a model, as well as a head.

However his policy and actions may be judged, it can scarcely be denied that, from his far-sighted, strong and single-minded government, and spiritual reforms based on the Council of Trent, came great and universal advantages in all fields, which until our own times continued to be enjoyed by the whole Church.

Chapter 4

PROTESTANTISM AND
EUROPEAN DIPLOMACY

At the Diet of Augsburg in 1530, the Emperor Charles V had rejected the "Confession" of Protestantism and ordered the restoration of Catholic worship in Germany to the exclusion of any other; yet only a quarter of a century later, after the "Interim" declared by the Emperor, with concessions to the Protestants and pending the resumption of the Council of Trent, Catholicism and Protestantism were officially recognized by the "Peace" of Augsburg in 1555: according to the slogan *Cuius regio, eius religio,* every ruler was granted the right to decide which religion was to be practiced in his territory.

When Pius V came to the Throne in 1566, Protestantism was continuing to gain ground in most of the German provinces. Luther had died in 1546, but Calvin, who did not die till 1564, had meanwhile built the heresiarch's revolt into a codified religion. The Emperor Maximilian II, who should have been the chief stay of the Church in Europe, was making matters worse by wavering between the religious traditions of his predecessors and the new ways of the reformers.

Elizabeth, whose hereditary right to the English Crown was not recognized by Pius IV, had caused schism to pass into official heresy and apostasy by having Parliament declare her supreme in spiritual as well as temporal matters and by imposing the new religion of "Thirty-Nine Articles of Faith" and a liturgy altered out of recognition upon the nation—and also upon Ireland; whilst Mary Stuart, deprived of the Crown of Scotland, but considered by many to be the rightful heir to the English throne, was the prisoner of Elizabeth at Lochleven.

France was virtually in the hands of the unscrupulous, Machiavellian regent, Catherine de Medici, mother of the young King Charles IX, and the Huguenots were threatening the country's religious and civil unity.

Spain, the most Catholic and united of European nations—and the most wealthy—comparatively immune from the worldly spirit of the Renaissance, was having trouble with the Netherlands where the King's envoy, the Duke of Alva, had only succeeded in aggravating the hostility fanned into revolt by Calvinists from Geneva; nor was Philip II's rule altogether worthy of a Catholic monarch.

Switzerland was in the grip of Calvinism. Scandinavia was largely lost to the Church. Poland was on the verge of schism.

To crown all, by rulers lacking in faith of some of Italy's States (theoretically independent but in practice under Spanish domination), the Pope had come to be looked on as little more than an Italian

prince among others, with small claim to spiritual,
let alone temporal allegiance.

The forthright, unworldly and, humanly speaking, undiplomatic character and policy of Pius V
must have made many in the Roman Curia and
diplomatic circles wonder how the new Pope would
go about handling the European situation. This very
unworldliness and absolute detachment from all
earthly interests, seeing things as they really were
from the heights of his intense and prolonged supernatural contemplation, were, on the other hand,
what enabled Pope Pius to overcome one obstacle
after another put in the way of his spiritual sovereignty or impeding the exercise of his temporal
government. His sole claim, declared and appar-
ent, was to marshal the Church's forces for God's
honor and glory, and the true well-being of Christian people.

Within a year, his diplomatic activities in all direc-
tions were such as to astonish professional diplomats and politicians. When some expressed surprise
that the Pope should spend more time in prayer
and meditation than in giving audiences and receiving counsellors, Pius' reply was that more works
are achieved in this world by two joined hands than
by any means of warfare.

In his dealings with the Emperor Maximilian,
and for affairs in various European countries, Pope
Pius V greatly relied on Cardinal Commendone,
one of the ablest and most experienced diplomats
who had served under previous pontiffs. The "Peace
of Augsburg," far from quieting religious conflict,

had produced such a multiplying of religions that the Emperor found himself seriously embarrassed. He put forward the preposterous solution that all Protestant sects should be suppressed, but not Lutheranism, which alone should be authorized so as to give citizens free choice between not more than two religions. Pope Pius' reaction may be imagined. His directives and warnings became more and more severe until at last, unable any longer to countenance the Faith being compromised by Emperor and princes, he decided on an extreme use of his absolute sovereignty and notified the legate, Cardinal Commendone, that Maximilian should be declared deposed if persisting in his errors and policy. All the Holy See's representatives were to leave Vienna. The Legate, judging such action might draw hitherto disunited Protestants into dangerously hostile unity, did not carry out the Pope's orders. In not insisting, Pius showed not only his trust in Cardinal Commendone but also his humility and wisdom by admitting that, in a matter of such import, another's judgment could be better than his own.

Pius V's endeavors to extirpate heresy in Prussia were successful. So great was the people's respect for him that in Danzig they let themselves be persuaded first into giving back to the Dominicans the church and monastery that had been taken from them, then allowing them license to preach throughout the city. As a consequence, many whom the new doctrines had taken by surprise were led back to the practice of their religion. From then on the

Dominicans were able to preach, with similar results, all over Prussia, the Pope backing them up by sending substantial aid, also for much-needed corporal works of mercy. The numbers abjuring heresy eventually grew to such proportions that the Dominicans were presently unable to receive all the converts and had to call in others to help them.

The King of Poland was pressing the Holy See for a dissolution of his marriage on a pretext not unlike that of Henry VIII's, namely, that the queen could not bear him a son and he had to have an heir. Several Polish Bishops with ambitious aims and infected by Protestantism, instead of restraining the king were, "in the interests of the State," backing him up. The king's family and court, too, were leaning towards the unorthodox teachings of the Socinians[1] at that time being persuasively propagated in Poland. Perceiving the danger of a national schism on a scale such as that of England, Pius V sent Cardinal Commendone to the Polish king who, however, tried by every means to win the Cardinal over to his side. Instead, the experienced Legate, together with the few Bishops that had remained faithful, prevailed upon the others to reaffirm their orthodoxy and hold a council, at which Cardinal Commendone spoke so convincingly of the dissensions and persecutions suffered in England as to persuade them against bringing about a similar break with Rome.

---

[1] Lelio and Fausto Sozzini, Italian heretics, subsequently banished from Poland, had drawn many into their sect that took Scripture as sole rule of faith whilst denying the doctrine of the Holy Trinity.

Shaken but unconverted, the king feigned conviction. But no sooner had the Legate left the country than he began repeating his requests for the Holy See to allow introduction of Protestant practices such as a married clergy, Communion under two kinds and freedom for religious sectaries to practice and propagate their several cults. The king's requests were not really made in the hope of obtaining them, as he claimed, for the good of the people, but rather with the design of making the Pope appear unreasonably intransigent by his inevitable refusals, thus gaining popular favor for himself and for the dissolution of his marriage.

Realizing this, Pope Pius intervened directly by letter to those he knew were abetting the king, but without being aware that the Archbishop of Gneszno, chief among them, had meanwhile secretly apostatized.

Again Pius sent Cardinal Commendone to Poland, where this time he found support in the Jesuits who had come into the country to help remedy things; and enough influence was brought to bear upon clergy and people to save the nation from general schism and apostasy. The papal Legate did not leave Poland before getting an official declaration from the king, whose wife had meanwhile died, that he would remain faithful to the religion of his fathers.

The progress of the "Reform" in Scotland was furthered by the greed and ambition of many of the Scottish nobles, and by slack ecclesiastical discipline, owing partly to the Crown's interference in

Church appointments and affairs. The country was also divided into two political factions, one favoring an alliance with Catholic France, the other with England.

Mary Queen of Scots wrote to Pius V of her plight and the Pope wrote back to her, appealing also on her behalf to various European powers. "For fear that our sins make us unworthy of being heard," ran part of a letter to the young queen during the first year of his reign, "we have had recourse to the prayers of many religious and priests. We would willingly sacrifice our life for you." Unable to travel to Scotland because of his age and duties, the Pope told Mary Stuart he had sent an envoy to do whatever he could for her.

When Mary escaped from Lochleven Castle in 1568 only to find prolonged reimprisonment at Fotheringay, which was to end in her execution at the hands of her "good Cousin" Elizabeth, Pope Pius continued his efforts on her behalf, though with a certain reserve toward one who could appear to be a rival claimant to the English throne.

At first, Pius V, as his predecessor Pius IV, had entertained some hope of Elizabeth's conversion and encouraged certain projects in this regard. But once finding she was not to be trusted, he took the view that she was "a delinquent wearing a crown" and made public reference to her as a "pretended queen."

On the other hand, events in Mary's life, and her third marriage to the Earl of Bothwell, had made Rome diffident of her cause. Pope Pius himself appears to have regained full confidence in her from

reassurances reaching him through diplomatic chan-
nels, and from Mary's sincerity and piety. Yet he still
felt it necessary to encourage her, through her Paris
envoy, to persevere and not weaken in her attach-
ment to the Holy See. In a letter sent to Pius at the
end of 1569, Mary told the Pope there was no truth
in the report made to Philip of Spain that she was
wavering: deprived of the means of Catholic worship, she had listened to the prayers of a Protestant
minister—that was all. She humbly asked penance if
she had erred in so doing. This removed all diffi-
dence, and Pius now wrote unreservedly that he was
certain no threat would ever be able to sever her
from the Communion and obedience of the Holy
See. Still hoping in help for her from the kings of
France and Spain, he declared himself convinced
that her misfortunes had come upon her for having
kept and defended the Catholic Faith, and consoled
her with the words of Christ: "Happy are they that
suffer persecution for justice's sake."

When Cardinal Inquisitor, Pius had granted certain English priests faculties for re-admitting schis-
matics into the Catholic Church, the only condition
then having been to refrain from reception of the
Protestant eucharist. In 1567, as Pope, he made the
further, more rigorous condition of non-attendance
at Protestant services. The effects of this were positive, some of the priests in question reporting an
end to considerable wavering. More and more
Catholics, mostly of the older generation, refused
to take part in Anglican worship, professing their
faith courageously before magistrates and willingly

accepting penalties and imprisonment; but they expressed their fears for their children and the younger ones listening to heretical preaching.

Writing in 1561 to the Cardinal Protector of England, Cardinal Morone, the Welsh priest and jurist Dr. Morus Clynnog (one-time confidante of Cardinal Pole and future warden of Rome's English hospice) had told him it was quite untrue the English, as was rumored, could not bear the thought of a foreign monarch, which restoration of Catholicism by force of arms would mean: many felt it were "better to go to Heaven under foreign leadership than be dragged to Hell by an enemy at home." By the end of that decade, hopes in Mary Stuart had risen high and it was thought that, if help could come from Spain, she might in a short time be made queen. But Spain had enough on her hands dealing with Moors and Marranos, as well as the revolt in the Netherlands; and English Catholics had scruples (a factor brought out by the historian Charles Edwards) about fighting an anointed prince until such time as she had been declared a heretic by Rome. Part of the mission of the Cambridge theologian Dr. Nicholas Morton, penitentiary at St. Peter's and warden of the English hospice, who travelled to England as Pius' envoy in 1569, was therefore to sound the Catholics of the realm concerning the question of Elizabeth's possible excommunication.

Dr. Morton returned to Rome shortly before the rising organized by the Northern Earls who had written to the Pope for support in their endeavor to free Mary. Pius had replied, urging them to be constant and courageous in the event of their having to shed their blood for the Faith and the Pope's authority.

On learning of the failure of the rising after the momentary triumph in Durham, and that Elizabeth had ruthlessly sentenced nearly a thousand persons to torture and death, Pius V was almost alone in raising his voice in protest and condemnation of the queen's action. Most European monarchs remained silent for reasons of political interest.

Pope Pius received the counsels of English refugees in Rome, almost all in favor of restoration by force of arms, but did not allow himself to be determined by them knowing they had not been in direct contact with England for some time. But on Dr. Morton's return toward the end of 1569 he had the English queen advised that proceedings according to the Church's canons were to be instituted against her. The papal envoy's evidence, anyway, along with that of other Englishmen proscribed for their religion, 12 in all, including a number of those resident in the English hospice, served as basis in drawing up the Bull of excommunication *Regnans in excelsis*. The 12 were formally questioned about something known to all; but legal proof was required by legal proceedings.[2]

In February 1570, after spending days in prayer and fasting, Pius V finally put his signature to the Bull placing Elizabeth under the ban of the Church. The Bull was founded upon the Supreme Pontiff's right to preserve the members of the one true Church from peril of corruption, and to punish apostates. By virtue of the powers conferred on him, the Pope declared the English queen guilty of heresy, and of upholding heresy, thereby incurring excommunication from the fold and forfeiting her pretended right to the crown of England. Her subjects were no longer bound by their oath of allegiance to her and under pain of excommunication might not themselves lend her obedience.

The Emperor Maximilian, influenced by the English ambassador, wrote urging the Pope even then not to have the Bull promulgated. The King of Spain, complaining he had not been consulted, objected that zeal was not enough to guarantee success and that such an act would worsen the situation of English Catholics.

But Pius' mind was made up. Rome had waited more than a decade, during which one appeal after another had reached Elizabeth in vain. Crowned according to Catholic rites, she had sworn to govern as a Catholic monarch. But almost immediately violating her coronation oath, and repudiating

---

[2] They were questioned as to whether Elizabeth had usurped the authority of the Church's head in England. It was not maintained either in the acts of the process, or in the Pope's final sentence, that she had usurped the title. Protestant polemics inaccurately maintained this, misinterpreting the Bull's relative passage: *"supremi Ecclesiae capitis locum in omni Angliae eiusque praecipium auctoritatem monstruose sibi usurpans. . ."* whilst accusing Rome of ignorance and inaccuracy. Yet Elizabeth *had* virtually usurped the title as well as the authority—Protestants themselves, for one thing, declaring she had the same power as the Pope, making her self-styled head.

the Pope's authority, she had begun to destroy the Catholic Faith and persecute the Church. The chief reason Pius V gave for having the Bull published was the prayers of English Catholics. His intention, he told the Spanish ambassador, was to give courage; and as the Catholics of England had requested justice against Elizabeth, he could not in conscience refuse.

Possibly this was why the Bull was not published with the usual formalities, but simply made known in England. A number of copies were sent, care of the Italian London banker Ridolfi, reaching the capital three months later. As everyone knows, one of these was fixed to the door of Lambeth Palace by Felton, who willingly paid for his action with his life.

Mitigation, withdrawal, suspension of the Bull were in turn urged by various European sovereigns, as Elizabeth had Parliament pass a further series of laws against her Catholic subjects, and it was objected the Bull was failing in its effect. But there is no doubt that *Regnans in excelsis* was at the same time producing just the effect Pius V had intended, namely, that of giving English Catholics new certainty and strength to resist the queen's tyrannous enforcement of heresy upon the nation.

A plan was devised to oblige Elizabeth to abdicate without recourse to arms by publishing the Bull in Spain and France and have these countries suspend all commerce with England. Pius V approved; but the Spanish king thought it impracticable.

Pretending to despise the Bull, Elizabeth was

secretly working through the Emperor Maximilian to get it withdrawn, aware as she was that growing numbers of her people were disaffected, and utterly refusing to attend the new divine service in English.[3] The Pope's comment was that if the queen attributed such importance to the Bull, why would she not return to the Church? If she gave it no weight, why did she worry so much about it? Pius added, that if the only way of calming heated passions were by shedding his own blood he would more greatly rejoice in that than in possessing the papal dignity.

Finding her efforts and threats of no avail with the Emperor, Elizabeth changed her tactics by launching a campaign of ridicule and defamation against Pope Pius. Bullinger and others were employed to write government propaganda denouncing the "shameful, lying Bull" and papist Bishops. Evidently ordered to alter a point in his manuscript, the author seems to have done so in one place, but forgot to in another—for in the same book the Bishops are first described as being treated well and better than they deserve, then as languishing and dying in prison solely on account of their malevolence. The right claimed in the Bull by the Pope, up to that time accepted by every crowned head in Europe, was represented as a threat to the security of sovereigns, an argument still being used a century later by Protestants as a pretext for violating

---

[3] Referred by the (Protestant) Bishop of Carlisle to the Earl of Sussex, October, 1570.

the rights of Catholics.

The Bull has been generally defended by Catholic writers who have granted that St. Pius V did the only possible thing left for the head of the Church to do in regard to Elizabeth and the whole complicated question, after every means had been tried.

Nevertheless, Pius V's policy has been called in question even by Catholics of repute and *Regnans in excelsis* regarded as an error of judgment—this opinion found, for example, in Donald Attwater's *Dictionary of the Popes,* published in 1939 with the Westminster *Imprimatur.* This dictionary quotes Pius IX as saying that nowadays "No one thinks of the right of deposing princes formerly exercised by the Holy See, and the Supreme Pontiff thinks of it less than anybody." (May these remarkable words in regard to a right no longer exercised have had an ironic note, as well as a plaintive ring?) *Regnans* is held by Mr. Attwater to have aggravated controversies, weakened the Catholic body and originated suspicions about Catholic civil loyalty persisting to this day.

Criticism of this kind recently reached extremes in Patrick McGrath's attempt to argue, in *The Tablet,* marking the Bull's 400th anniversary in 1970, that Pius used "the wrong weapon, in the wrong way at the wrong time." St. Pius V's action, according to Mr. McGrath, not only failed to achieve its purpose of removing a heretical queen but was second only to the Gunpowder Plot in contributing to the anti-Catholic tradition in England. Pius V moreover took no account of "European realities," and his "mistaken and out-of-date" policy toward Elizabeth was owing to his not understanding the situation in England.

That the Catholics of England had divided views over their allegiance to Elizabeth, and whether she was *ipso facto* a heretic for having broken her coronation oath, no one denies. The queen's own Council was divided, and there were aristocratic, conservative Protestants who favored Mary Stuart, though clearly not for religious reasons. But what evidence is there that the Bull *Regnans in excelsis* weakened the Catholic body? It may have made cowards of some, and confirmed others in cowardice; but many more were given the necessary strength to stay away from the new services despite the cruel penalties, as other Protestant Bishops attested besides the one already cited. Catholic civil loyalty was made suspect, not by the decisive action of a saintly Roman pontiff but by the ambitious, persecuting policy of an apostate temporal monarch from the outset of her reign, long before *Regnans in excelsis* was at last, on reliable witness, drawn up against her. Nor was the Bull a mere legal document, a "weapon" used only for the pragmatic purpose of removing a heretical queen. By excommunicating Elizabeth, Pius V, in the most solemn way possible, declared her, by her own acts and pronouncements, no longer of the Catholic Communion; as a consequence—whatever theologians may competently say about the nature and extent of the inherent right of deposition, or canonists about the correctness, interpretation and application of the Bull's clauses—the English queen became disqualified from governing the nation according to a principle which, though questioned and diminished, cannot be historically denied. As to *Regnans* failing in its effect upon Elizabeth, for that Pius V was not to blame—but the Emperor, Catholic in name but not in conscience or practice, and those sovereigns who kept silence and did nothing, for lesser political reasons, instead of joining with the head of Christendom and giving combined support to his action, were at fault.

As an impartial, objective judgment, von Pastor's conclusion should be referred to, although it still leaves something to be desired as a final explanation (but God knows): "It was an era in which the Pope's surveyance over temporal sovereigns was disappearing, whilst their subjects had not yet the awareness or achieved the means of uniting on a legal basis against the whims of local tyranny. In this respect, the Bull *Regnans in excelsis* of Pius V shows up, as in a shaft of light, the whole 16th century religious situation."

Chapter 5

LEPANTO: THE HOLY ALLIANCE
AGAINST THE TURKS

"The Turkish successes began in the middle of
the XI century. They ended in the XVI. Selim the
Sot came to the throne of Othman and St. Pius
V to the throne of the Apostle...The battle of
Lepanto arrested forever the danger of Moham-
medan invasion in the South of Europe—and
Lepanto was won by prayer..." wrote John Henry
Cardinal Newman.

As early as 1073 Pope St. Gregory VII conceived
(but did not live to carry out) the first Crusade.
Since the 7th century, the Holy Places of Palestine
had been in the hands of Mohammedans, and the
Seljuk Turks—after capturing Jerusalem—were
threatening Constantinople and the Eastern Empire.

The medieval Crusades (1099-1270), though not
always successful and marred by lack of discipline,
intrigue and political divisions, did keep the West
from invasion and staved off conquest of the East.

A united Christian league against the Turks was
what was in the mind of St. Catherine of Siena
in pacifying the warring Italian States and bringing
Pope Gregory XI back to Rome, ending the papal

exile at Avignon in 1377. But the ideal of a Christendom united under Pope and Emperor had been doomed by the "Golden Bull" of Charles IV in 1354, that marked the rise of excessive nationalism. The great schism of the West (1378-1417), with lawful popes at Rome and schismatic rivals continuing at Avignon, further prevented realization of St. Catherine's aim.

The need for a new Crusade was indeed realized by succeeding popes, in a better position than others to know the perils of national divisions which the united Turks took full advantage of. Little was effected, however; and in 1453 Constantinople finally fell to the armies of Mahomet II. This meant the end of the Byzantine Empire which for centuries had providentially barred Mohammedan entrance to Europe from the East.

Calixtus III appealed in vain to several European countries in an endeavor to get the Turks driven out of Constantinople. Pius II's noble efforts ended in failure and his death—all were too occupied with their own affairs. Paul II was unsuccessful, the Turks overrunning Greece in 1470. In 1480, during the Pontificate of Sixtus IV, Turkish troops landed at Otranto in southern Italy. Fruitless attempts were made by Innocent VIII to defeat the Turks in Europe. Leo X's appeals met with promises, but no support, from sovereigns wanting to get papal approval for their own ends.

Pius V was the Pope to whom fell the task of carrying out, at long last, the ideal that culminated in the greatest naval victory of history.

When the Turks succeeded in disembarking at Otranto, murdering the archbishop in his cathedral, martyrizing 800 men, and carrying off women and children into slavery, Mahomet II had boasted to the world that he would top St. Peter's dome with the Crescent Moon and wind the Pope's head in a turban. The failure of the Emperor Maximilian's attempt, in 1566, the first year of Pius V's reign, to wrest some Hungarian territory from the Turks who had conquered most of the country, weakened Catholic morale and resistance. Moreover, the Turkish fleet was practically master of the Mediterranean, making it said that if the Turk was terrible by land he was invincible by sea.

The first check to Turkish sea power had come in 1565 with Malta's valiant defense, against tremendous odds, led by the Grand Master of the Sovereign Order of St. John of Jerusalem, Jean de la Valette. But the cost of victory had been so high in loss of men, ships and ruined fortifications that the Knights were thinking of abandoning Malta lest a further Turkish onslaught might mean defeat.

Pope Pius V strongly encouraged de la Valette to hold on in his defense of this vital island outpost of Christendom, and at the same time sought help for him from Spain and Portugal, and the Venetian Republic. He provided money and architects to rebuild the forts and founded a new capital, from then on known as Valetta.[1]

The check given to the Turkish fleet by Malta determined the Sultan to turn his attention to the Grecian archipelago. From the start of his pontificate, Pius V, whose thoughts were not of war but of peace, had nevertheless seen the need for a common call to arms on the part of European sovereigns and peoples, as well as the prayer and penance necessary to defeat the enemy. "By the penance of believing peoples, God's anger may be appeased and there will be hope in His all-powerful aid," he proclaimed. Spain and Venice, the greatest European sea powers, but also rivals, gave evasive replies to the Pope's first appeals for them to come into a joint crusade; consequently the Turks easily succeeded in capturing one of the Greek islands, whose inhabitants were subjected to barbarous cruelties. They then threatened the Italian port of Ancona. But owing to the Pope's prompt intervention they were repelled. In 1570, when a peremptory demand for Venice to hand over the Republic's most treasured Mediterranean possession, Cyprus, was equally bluntly refused, the Turks attacked the island.

Now it was Venice's turn to appeal to the Pope for moral and material aid in furthering an alliance with other powers against the Turkish aggressor. This was no easy task, on account of divergent political and economic interests; but it had from the

---

[1] By papal Brief, work on this task was allowed on Sundays and holidays. A bronze bust of St. Pius V was later set up over the main gateway of Valetta.

In March 1966, the fourth centenary of Valetta's foundation, the government issued a series of postage stamps, the second of which, of the value of 3d, shows Pius V with three Church dignitaries, and his coat-of-arms.

outset been Pius V's steady aim. So now, knowing
there was no alternative but to give battle, he set
the example himself by ordering the rebuilding and
reequipment of the little papal fleet, nearly wiped
out in an encounter some years ago. The new ships
were to be constructed on more efficient and up-
to-date lines—and the Pope gave the order to Venice,
which at that time had the finest arsenal in the
world.

Meanwhile, Pius pursued his work of persuasion
for the various Christian countries, first and foremost Spain, to unite with Venice in an alliance.

"Coming from regions beyond the Caucasus," Pope
Pius publicly proclaimed, tracing the history of the
Turkish menace, "these barbarous and little-known
peoples became by degrees more and more daring.
Giving themselves up to the most shameless brigand-
age, they began their armed invasions of neighbor-
ing Christian provinces, Thrace and Cappadocia,
as far as the banks of the Tigris and Euphrates.
After eating up almost the whole of Asia, the Turks
got possession of Constantinople and invaded
Greece. The two great powers of Egypt and Syria
fell into their hands. Soliman recently conquered
part of Hungary, took the island of Rhodes, be-
sieged Malta and occupied the island of Chios by
trickery. Selim, itching to extend his tyrannous and
rapacious sway still further, now decides on assault-
ing Cyprus."

The Pope's words everywhere sounded the alarm
and stirred to united action. Still the different countries of Europe, for one reason or another, were

not in a position to respond. Only the King of Spain, whilst not consenting to an explicit alliance with Venice, condescended to allow a part of his fleet stationed at Messina to join the crusade in aid of Cyprus. But lack of agreement and little will to fight among the allies delayed the fleet's arrival.

In September 1570, Turkish troops disembarked on the island whose capital, Nicosia, fell with the savage massacre of all 20,000 inhabitants. Only the fortified port of Famagusta held out, until August of the following year.

During the months that followed, the tenacity, diplomatic skill and absolute certainty of Pius V that he was serving the interests of the Church and his imperiled Christian peoples saved the alliance from altogether foundering. Even when news reached him that the Spanish ships had withdrawn to their base, leaving the papal and Venetian galleys helpless, and there seemed little hope any more, Pius did not give into what might have been taken for an adverse fate which there was no avoiding. He had too great a trust in supernatural means not to make full use of them: putting all other affairs aside, he spent some days wholly in prayer and fasting. Then he threw himself anew into the task of reorganizing a fresh crusade on morally and materially surer and vaster lines.

Maximilian's cool reception of papal envoys whilst lavishing honors upon Protestant and Turkish missions prompted Pius to send Cardinal Commendone to Vienna to gauge the Emperor's sincerity and true attitude. Assured at least of Maximilian's formal backing of the new alliance, the Pope sent legates to all European courts, and to the kings of France and Portugal in particular.

The former gave as excuse for not taking part a commercial treaty signed with Turkey, in the interests of Christian peace; the latter said he was ready to fight the Turks, but on his own.

Writing to express his indignation that a descendent of faithful Catholic sovereigns should think of entering into such negotiations with "an inhuman tyrant and declared enemy of Our Lord Jesus Christ," Pope Pius told the young French king that he was committing a serious error, in forgetting that one may never do evil in order to accomplish good.

The French king, together with Catherine de Medici, then tried to dissuade the Venetians from taking part in the crusade and joined with Elizabeth of England (who herself made vain efforts to negotiate an alliance with Constantinople) in accusing Pius V of wanting to destroy Protestants more than vanquish the Turks.

Philip II of Spain in the end had the loyalty to refuse to listen to advisers urging him to put the interests of his own kingdom above the plans of the Pope who, they said, was aiming to subject all Europe to Rome. Declaring the Church's cause, on the contrary, above that of his own temporal concerns, the Spanish sovereign sent word to Pius V that he committed his country's fate to the prayers of the Supreme Pontiff and the protection of Almighty God.

Overjoyed, and giving thanks to God, Pius at once

convoked the representatives of Spain and Venice in Rome, appointing a commission of Cardinals to draw up the terms of the new alliance. His joy was short-lived: Spaniards and Venetians soon began organizing forces each to their own advantage, and all was once more delayed.

In a forthright letter to King Philip, Pius asked him to see that his envoys behaved themselves in a way worthy of the religion they professed to believe in. This had its effect; but even then an obstacle remained: one half the total cost was to be paid by Spain, two thirds of the remainder to be borne by Venice, and one third by the Pope. There was not enough money in the papal treasury for the Holy See to fulfill its part. This difficulty was at length solved by the Pope's authorizing Philip II to tax the privileged Spanish clergy, who had for some time enjoyed exemption. Taxes were not otherwise levied; only voluntary offerings were asked of the people.

There was lastly the important choice of a commander-in-chief. The appointment of Don Juan of Austria, son of the Emperor Charles V and half-brother to the King of Spain, proved acceptable to all. He was only twenty-four, but to suitably neutral lineage were added winning personal qualities. He had shown exceptional valor in previous operations, and he was known to be, above all, a true and fervent Catholic.

Mark Anthony Colonna was a second time in command of the papal galleys; the veteran Sebastian Venier of the Venetian.

Meantime Pope Pius ordered extraordinary prayers, day and night, in all convents and monasteries of Rome, besides public prayers and penitential processions in which he himself took part, despite his overwhelming labors. He invited the Cardinals to fast once a week and give extra alms to obtain God's merciful and all-powerful help in the great and momentous enterprise.

Pius himself fasted three days a week—this was referred to in ambassadors' reports of the time—and continued to spend hours each day in prayer. Miracles of physical healing and spiritual grace became frequent and so well-known that the Turkish Sultan declared that he feared the prayers of Pius V more than all the forces at the Emperor's command.

In a dispatch sent from Madrid in September 1570, when the alliance appeared to have been compromised by disagreement and delay, the Venetian ambassador reported learning from the papal envoy of Pius' express desire that, in the event of his dying before all parties had on every point concurred, those clauses already agreed should be signed, it being imperative for the good of Christendom that the various powers concerned should ally themselves as best they could, and as quickly as possible.

By the early summer of 1571, ailing as Pope Pius was and often enduring great physical pain, hope that had been so dim the year before was once again bright, though problems remained: rumors persisted that, in spite of all, Venice was seeking a means of making peace with the Turks; and the Venetian ambassador himself expressed his fears that Don Juan might have to engage his ships that year not in the Levant but off the coasts of Barbary.

The offensive and defensive Holy Alliance against the Turk was at length sworn and signed by the three contracting parties—Spain; Venice, Genoa and other Italian States; the Knights of Malta and the Holy See—in May 1571.

The document, drawn up in 24 articles, showed the clear and resolute mind of Pius V. Nothing was overlooked, no place allowed for prevarication. The Pope was to be sole arbiter in any difference that might arise between the allied powers. The question of ships, men and supplies to be furnished by each was dealt with in detail. All possibility of effective rivalry was this time ruled out. The allies were forbidden to arrange a separate peace, or truce. Pope Pius' skill as negotiator was still further revealed by his having a clause inserted that every important decision had to be made by majority resolution on the part of the League's three heads, to ensure avoidance of disagreements that had been the cause of delay and failure before.

A letter written in Pius V's own hand to the Grand Master of the Knights of Malta showed something of what the enterprise had cost him in labor and even passing discouragement, apart from aggravating the complaint he suffered from which was in another year to bring about his death. He could certainly have failed, the Pope admitted, so many were there on all sides seeking to make him succumb, had he not steadfastly put himself in the hands of the Saviour, who had said: "He that would follow me, let him deny himself."

In the Bull *Consueverunt* of 1569, Pius V had enjoined the prayer of the Holy Rosary as the most effective means against heresy. (The present way of saying the Rosary was laid down by Pope Pius in this Bull.) Now the Pope put the new crusade he had worked so long to inspire and organize under the protection of Our Lady Queen of the Most Holy Rosary.

Don Juan received the standard of the League, blessed by the Pope, from Cardinal Granvelle, viceroy of Naples, before proceeding to Messina. There, after a final council of war, at which Pius V's Nuncio was present, the Christian fleet prepared for departure. Sufficient information had come to hand concerning the Turks, who were known to be at their naval base of Lepanto, in the Gulf of Corinth.

Dominican, Franciscan and Jesuit religious embarked on each vessel to celebrate daily Masses to see that the soldiers and sailors fulfilled their religious duties and refrained from gambling, swearing and blasphemy, for which there were severest penalties. The Rosary was to be recited daily on each ship.

Even at this final stage there were hesitations, Don Juan's counsellors in particular doubting the advisability of attacking the Turks at sea when they had for so long proved their superiority. The plea of one of the Spanish commanders for prompt and unquestioning obedience to the Pope's wishes won the others, Don Juan professing full agreement.

As the entire fleet sailed out of Messina harbor from a brig anchored at the entrance, the Apostolic Nuncio gave the papal blessing to the crews of kneeling men on board each passing galley.

A serious incident on one of the Italian ships made for strained relations between Venier and Don Juan, whose advisers before long began speaking again of the risk in confronting the Turkish fleet, and of the far-reaching consequences for all Christendom if the enemy were to win. But Don Juan, to his great credit, resolutely kept to the agreement reached at Messina.

Then, from a Venetian frigate, the news was learnt of the fall of Famagusta: the treachery of the Turks towards its gallant defenders, and the horrible fate of their heroic leader, General Bragadin, who suffered being flayed alive without a groan, strengthened Don Juan in his resolve, and all in the conviction that the Turks must now be beaten and Famagusta avenged, at any cost.

At dawn on October 7, 1571, the allied Christian fleet lay at the mouth of the Gulf of Patras, unaware that the enemy, who had meanwhile left Lepanto, was no more than 14 miles off; neither were the Turks aware of how near the Christian fleet had come. At a last council of war that morning, Don Juan for the third time refused to heed the warnings of his counsellors. As it happened, the young Turkish commander-in-chief, Ali Pasha, also disregarding similar counsel, had confirmed the order to advance—but more from over-confidence and thirst for glory, Don Juan's motives being rather faith in Christ and obedience to the Pope, not unmixed with healthy youthful ambition. Thus the two fleets sighted each other unexpectedly at about ten miles' distance, off Cape Scrofa, after which could have been named the greatest sea battle in Christian history.

As soon as his ships were assembled in fighting formation, Don Juan boarded a swift vessel and passed from one to the other holding high his crucifix. He reminded all of the Plenary Indulgence granted by Pius V and assured them of victory, the men responding with cheers for the Pope and their commander-in-chief.

From the Turkish galleys came the din of shouting and crying, and the weird sounds of their war instruments; but there was silence on the Christian ships as Don Juan, appearing on the forecastle of the royal galley, lifted up the relics given him by Pope Pius, and soldiers and seamen knelt for the general Absolution and blessing imparted by the chaplains.

Don Juan then gave the signal for attack: the League standard of blue damask blessed by the Pope, to be hoisted only at the moment of joining battle, was seen fluttering aloft, the allied emblems embroidered in gold below the image of the crucified Saviour; and cries went up of "Victory! Victory! In the name of Christ!"

The victory that followed was not won without high cost: 7,500 Christian men perished, the greater part Venetian—but Italian history records with pride the sacrifice made by those of every region—and twelve galleys were sunk; but the Turks, as far as could be reckoned, lost 30,000 men, 8,000 were taken prisoner and all but 45 of their 270 ships sunk or captured, freeing thousands of Christian galley-slaves. The sea became red with blood and so littered with smoking wreckage and floating corpses that it was nearly impossible to row in any direction.

The battle's final stage was fought out between the two admiral ships amid a mass of attendant galleys so closely locked that it resembled a land combat, with Christian and Turkish soldiery alternately invading and being repelled from one another's galleys till at length the Turkish Commander's ship was overcome by a decisive thrust from Mark Anthony Colonna's and Don Juan's men. Ali Pasha himself was killed, and his head cut off. The Turkish flag was hauled down and a white, blood-stained banner from one of the League's ships hoisted in its place...

The battle of Lepanto was over at about 5 o'clock in the afternoon of Sunday, October 7. At that hour, Pius V, who had redoubled prayers and penances since the fleet's departure, was looking over accounts in the Vatican—several biographers relate—with the papal treasurer. All at once he rose and went over to a window, where he stayed gazing out toward the East. Then, turning round, his eyes alight with supernatural radiance, he exclaimed: "The Christian fleet is victorious!" and shed tears of thanksgiving to God.

It was not until two weeks and more later that

the Pope's prophetic vision was confirmed by a courier, delayed by storms at sea. Some say Pope Pius received the news with the words of Holy Scripture: The Lord has heard the prayers of the humble, and has not refused their request. Let these things be handed down from generation to generation, and all in future will give praise to God; others said that the words of the *Nunc dimittis*—Lord, now lettest Thou Thy servant depart in peace—were the ones that sprang to his lips before summoning those of his household who had gone to bed (it was late at night) to rise and join him in giving thanks.

St. Pius V attributed the winning of Lepanto, which decided the future of Europe, to the intercession of the Blessed Virgin. He ordered the invocation *Auxilium Christianorum*—Help of Christians—to be added to the Litany of Loreto, and decreed October 7 as the Feast of Our Lady of Victories. Gregory XIII transferred this Feast to the first Sunday of October, with the title of the Most Holy Rosary; Clement III extended it to the Universal Church.

Lepanto once and for all exploded the myth of Turkish sea invincibility and ended the threat of Mediterranean domination. It also marked the first time that men of every State and region of the then divided Italian peninsula—Genoa, Savoy, the Marches, Tuscany, Naples, Sicily as well as Venice—fought side by side in the name of the Christian Faith and Roman civilization. But the thoroughly impartial historian, Admiral de la Gravière, judged

Lepanto a Venetian victory as much as, and perhaps still more than, a Spanish one.

It was generally believed to be first and foremost a victory of prayer, the more wonderful in that the Ottoman fleet was not only somewhat superior numerically (though less well-equipped) but made up of one nation, whereas the Christian fleet was subject to all the drawbacks naturally consequent on different nationalities which might have proved disastrous but for the foresight of the Pope, unity of leadership and supernatural faith.

After the singing of the *Te Deum* in St. Peter's, Pius V, who spared nothing in lavishness and magnificence when it was for the honor and glory of God, surrounded by the Cardinals of the Sacred College gave an incomparable welcome to Mark Anthony Colonna, as well as to the Commander of the Knights of Malta who had sustained heavy losses in the battle.

The Roman Senate proclaimed: *"Adhuc viget virtus, flagrat amor, pollet pietas"*—now bravery triumphs, love reigns, piety flourishes. The ceiling of the Basilica of *S. Maria in Aracoeli* was decorated with the gold taken from Turkish galleys; and a great fresco was painted in the Vatican *Sala Regia* by Vasari.

To Don Juan, without whose clear-headed and brave leadership and youthful ardor, victory might not have been decisive, Pope Pius applied the scriptural text: *"Fuit homo missus a Deo, cui nomen erat Joannes"*—There was a man sent from God, whose name was John—promising him still greater honors. But he did not come to Rome. Returning to Spain, his welcome was not triumphant. He was even reproved for having exposed the King's fleet to too great a risk in proportion to the advantages gained, from which Venice had benefitted. He died in retirement a few years later. A statue was erected to his memory at Messina. To this day, great crowds gather during Holy Week to venerate his crucifix, which is kept in Barcelona Cathedral.

"Non virtus, non arma, non duces, sed Mariae Rosarium victores nos fecit"—Neither valor, nor arms, nor leaders, but the Rosary of Our Lady gave the victory. So Venice believed, and had publicly recorded. The veteran Commander Sebastian Venier, wounded in the battle, was later made Doge of Venice. In 1580, the skin of General Bragadin, Famagusta's heroic defender, was brought to the city from Constantinople and placed in an urn over a memorial erected to him in the great 12th century Dominican Basilica of Saints John and Paul. To the same Basilica were also transferred the mortal remains of Commander Venier. Today, in this magnificent specimen of sacred architecture standing in the midst of the city of lagoons, the visitor may therefore contemplate, with its chapel of St. Pius V, and of the Holy Rosary, much of Lepanto.

Tintoretto, Veronese, Titian and others commemorated the battle in paintings.

Cervantes, then an unknown Spanish writer, also wounded at Lepanto, proclaimed his belief in a victory of prayer in his novel *Don Quixote,* as have many other writers, including in our own day G. K.

Chesterton, with his "Ballad of Lepanto."

Pius V, who above the conflicting temporal interests of Spain and Venice had never ceased disinterestedly to stand for the higher, vaster spiritual concept of a European coalition against the Ottoman aggression, did not rest after the victory but endeavored to maintain and extend the alliance, sending Letters to the Emperor and various European rulers—even to Persian, Ethiopian and Arabian sovereigns.

But, with the Pope's death half a year later, the alliance was dissolved for all intents and purposes, though continuing to exist in name for awhile.

Chapter 6

THE ROMAN CATECHISM,
THE BREVIARY AND THE MISSAL

Some of the popes before St. Pius V had been incapable of bringing about spiritual reform owing to overwhelmingly adverse circumstances, others had been unmindful of it; one or two had done something to fight corruption and heresy and put down the spurious reforms that sprang up, pretending to do good and misleading the faithful. The Council of Trent not only gathered up the hitherto dispersed forces of true reform, inspired and led by martyrs and saints, such as St. Thomas More, St. John Fisher, St. Ignatius Loyola, St. Cajetan, St. Angela Merici—it further provided that its clear-cut decrees be carried out by laying down correspondingly severe penalties for default.

The renewal achieved by Pius V, based on the Council of Trent, was completed by his publication of the Roman Catechism, or Catechism of Trent. This was followed by the revision of the Roman Breviary, and the Missal.

The new Protestant theologians and most of the German universities were actively working against the Church, falsifying Holy Scripture to suit their purposes and rewriting their doctrines so as to give them a semblance of tradition and truthfulness. These theologians were patronized by many of the lesser princes interested in supporting heresy which, by creating divisions among the people, increased their own power. Protestantism also gave to each ruler control of religious matters within his own State, as of religious property. The Reformers identified their doctrines, in their turn, with the national interest, freedom of conscience and human progress; and the average Catholic was often deceived, having neither the time nor the mental equipment to check things for himself.

Pope Pius therefore entrusted the Jesuit Peter Canisius, famed for his learning and gentleness, with the task of composing a particular work to refute the falsehoods and expose the tactics of the Protestant theologians who in actual fact were striking at the heart of the Catholic Faith, the Real Presence of Christ in the Eucharist, and the priesthood. After consulting St. Philip Neri, among others, in Rome, St. Peter Canisius produced his *De Corruptelis Verbi Dei*—Concerning Alterations of the Word of God—which proved at once most successful. It was followed by other more general works on a wider scale which, as Pius V who was not in the habit of mincing words said, served "to confound the lies of heretics."

What was, however, still more necessary than these works brought out with papal approval for a specific purpose was one published in the Pope's own name and for the entire Church. Trent had urged the drawing up of a compendium of Christian doctrine in clearest terms as the best means of safeguarding the Faith for Catholic peoples bewildered by so many new and contradictory doctrines.

Particulary confusing were the propositions of Michael Baius, professor of Sacred Scripture at Louvain University. He claimed not only to be leading theology back to the Bible and patristic sources from whence it had strayed during the Middle Ages, but also thereby to be reconciling Catholicism with the new ideas that were flooding churches, schools and families through books, leaflets and popular songs, affecting people more than they were aware. A sort of semi-Lutheranism was the result, denying amongst other things that Sanctifying Grace was necessary for man to merit. A break with past tradition was implied by Baius' theories, which he defended, against St. Robert Bellarmine, quoting the early Fathers, especially St. Augustine, out of context and detached from their historical background.

Pius V had already come to grips with Baianism as Inquisitor. By his Bull *Ex omnibus afflictionibus,* of 1567, more than twenty propositions were condemned, but without their author being named; Pius with fatherly goodness fearing to drive him into formal heresy. But he judged the errors of Baius so serious and dangerous that he gave the Bull's decrees solemn approbation, instead of ordinary.

All the more insulting, therefore, was the "apology" Baius sent to Pope Pius complaining of being misunderstood and calling the Bull a calumny on account of which, and for failing to give due consideration to the teaching of the early Fathers, the Pope would suffer the consequences.

Pius V then followed the Bull up by a confirming Brief imposing perpetual silence on the Louvain professor and all defenders and propagators of his teachings. But not until a year later was Baius induced to sign an act of submission.[1]

The seed of a compendium of clearly stated Catholic teaching for the whole Church, as recommended by Trent, had immediately been sown during the second year of the Council. Progress had been made under Pius IV, who had entrusted the editing of a text to two Dominican Bishops. St. Charles Borromeo played a considerable part in seeing the work through, as also in the task of revising and publishing the Roman Breviary and Missal.

Pius V now gave orders for the Catechism to be completed as quickly as possible. To fill in the delay over final editing and printing, he had immediately published the *Bibliotheca Sancta* of Sixtus of Siena, setting out sure principles of Biblical study.

---

[1] Gregory XIII issued a second condemnation, and Baius died reconciled to the Church. His ideas were revived, though, the following century by Jansenius, Bishop of Ypres, from whom came Jansenism, which proposed reforming the Church on its own lines and by a return to primitive practices. Defended by certain French Bishops, and by Pascal, Jansenism was several times revived, and several times condemned by the Popes, until receiving a final death blow in 1713 from Clement XI. It survived as a sect, known as the "Old Roman Catholics," in Holland.

After conclusive examination by various commissions, the Catechism was at last issued in 1566, under the Latin title of *Catechismus ex decreto concilii Tridentini, ad parochos*. Addressed in the name of the Supreme Pontiff principally to parish priests, the Trent Catechism gave a most clear exposition of the Catholic Faith, dogma and morals, providing at the same time the fundamental elements of theology in a way that could easily be taught. This partly accounted for its immediate success, the extent of which could be gauged from Protestant reaction: the Huguenots among others heaped violent abuse on it, loud in their protests against "that odious and execrable Roman cabala."

Besides having the Catechism translated into the chief European languages, Pius V followed up publication by ensuring that the Catholic Bishops would indeed base their teaching on it and in turn have it taught. In 1571, the Pope still further issued a Bull recommending the Bishops to set up sodalities for this special purpose.

To Pius V also fell the task, taken up but not completed by his predecessors, of revising the Breviary, or Divine Office, which members of the clergy are bound to say daily, under pain of mortal sin. In the course of time, since the last revision by Gregory VII, various versions of the Breviary had come into use, cutting out or putting in things according to individual whim. Many of the clergy had hastily adopted the new and unauthorized abridged Breviary composed by Cardinal Quignonez. In some places, each Bishop devised his own particular

Breviary as he fancied, making the number of differing offices a confusing and disintegrating element in the Catholic Communion of prayer and praise offered in one and the same way to one and the same God, everywhere in the Latin Church. This unauthorized variety, allowing personal considerations to predominate over discipline and unity, Pius affirmed, was the cause of divine worship being upset and of the laxity and ignorance rife among the clergy: many gave scandal by the indecorous way they allowed rites to be carried out; not a few, discouraged, had given up saying any Breviary whatever.

In the Bull *Quod a nobis* of 1568, Pius V explained his reasons and principles regarding revision of the Breviary, which was to bind all except those who could show they had been using an Office approved by the Holy See for at least two hundred years, dating back to purer times before the introduction of novelties and arbitrary individual deviations. Thus, with wisdom and charity, the Holy See at the same time respected tradition and proscribed innovation.

The psalter and Scriptures once more came into their own with the revised Roman Breviary of Pius V. Former efforts to make due use in the West of the writings of the early Greek Fathers were furthermore taken into account. Persuaded that the work of the Council of Trent, which had condemned the heresies of the time and proclaimed the Church's true teaching, should be completed by a demonstration of the unity of dogmatic tradition in the

East and West, and of the Middle Ages with antiquity, the Pope decreed inclusion, for the first time, in the public worship of the Universal Church of the four Greek Doctors St. Athanasius, St. Basil, St. Gregory of Nazianzen and St. John Chrysostom, side by side with the four Latins, St. Augustine, St. Ambrose, St. Jerome and St. Gregory the Great. (It may be noted that Pius V, however, forbade Latin priests to say Mass in Greek, and Greek priests to say Mass in Latin).

The clergy of most countries welcomed the revised Breviary, although the French were slow in accepting it. Gregory XIII and Sixtus V, who succeeded Pius V and carried on his work, made some alterations which were criticized by St. Robert Bellarmine, among others. Pius V's achievement endured, so much so that two centuries later it was summed up as follows in the writings of Grancolas: "If in the 9th century the Roman Breviary deserved such praise as to be ranked above every other, it was made to appear again all the more brightly on St. Pius V's re-presenting it."

The Roman Breviary underwent some further subsequent modifications, but St. Pius X brought it back almost wholly to the text laid down by St. Pius V.

Revision of the Breviary was necessarily followed by that of the Missal. There was some variety of Mass rites in the West: apart from the ancient Milanese or Ambrosian, and the slightly differing usages of a few religious orders as the Carthusian and Dominican, Spain had the Mozarabic, France the Gallican and England the Sarum (the Bangor, Exeter and Hereford variants were done away with by order of Henry VIII). None of these departed substantially from the old Roman rite, which had taken on definite and final form early in the 5th century, with the building of the first Christian churches, after the Mass had emerged from the catacombs and it became possible, thanks to the Emperor Constantine, to worship in public edifices.[2] But divergences of relatively recent growth—from one nation to another, and even from diocese to diocese—had become an unsettling factor if not a threat to unity of faith, worship, doctrine and morals. The Protestant innovations, among others, substitution of liturgical Latin by the national idiom in the Mass and sacred rites, had at length seriously compromised unity; and Luther had said that when the Mass should be overthrown the papacy itself would be overcome.

As a counteractant and safeguard, Trent had ordered everywhere to be kept the ancient rites in the original languages—Latin in the West, Greek in the East, with a few other Eastern liturgies, admitted

---

[2] Gregory the Great in the 6th century only substituted the *Kyrie* for a previously recited litany and altered the position of the *Pater Noster*. The Canon was already fixed by his time, and never since underwent the least modification. The care with which St. Pius V, and all preceding and successive popes, took in preserving the Canon inviolate was because it most clearly shows the Mass as Sacrifice renewing and perpetuating that offered by Christ on Calvary, doctrine attacked by Protestant innovators who wanted but a memorial of the Supper.

and approved by the Holy See, for centuries in the Communion of the Roman Church, Mother and Mistress of all churches.

But even the decrees of the Council of Trent, greatest in a thousand years since that of Nicea called to combat Arianism, could have ended in sterility. Such a danger had fortunately been forestalled; for it was during the long-drawn-out preparations for the great Council, in which the English Cardinal Pole had a part, that Pope Paul III had instituted the permanent Congregation of the Universal Inquisition (or Holy Office, now of the Doctrine of the Faith) as supreme guardian and judge for the entire Church in matters of faith and morals. Formerly Inquisitor General of this Congregation, Pius V gave more detailed definition to its work, to which he assigned first place. The disorders and disunity disfiguring the Church had allowed the disaster of heretical reforms to overtake Christendom, and by combatting and clearly condemning these false doctrines the Pope dealt a deathblow to the malady.

The opening words of the Bull *Quo primum tempore,* posted upon the portals of St. Peter's on July 29, 1570, announced Pius V's intentions in unequivocal terms, as far as the liturgy of the Mass was concerned: "*...cum unum in Ecclesia Dei psallendi modum, unum Missae ditum esse maxime deceat...*"—"as it is most fitting that the Church should have one way of praising God, and one rite for the celebration of Mass..." One Mass was laid down for all, to have universally binding force in perpetuity, with the exception—as with the Breviary—of rites continuously in use, approved by the Holy See, for at least two hundred years. These ancient rites were not merely allowed but encouraged to continue; but should conformity to the new ordinance of the revised Missal now promulgated be preferred, instead of the lawful exception, permission could be sought and obtained. The Ambrosian, Carthusian, Dominican and one or two other variants of the Latin rite thus peaceably continued, as of course, the ancient Eastern liturgies—the Byzantine, Alexandrian, Antiochian, Armenian and Chaldean—in some respects still older than the Roman.

Unity and purity of faith, worship, doctrine and morals were thus safeguarded by uniformity of rite and language in the West, as in the East, with due exceptions in regard to sure tradition and antiquity. It was furthermore of the greatest benefit to the Universal Church that any alterations whatsoever in the liturgies were reserved to the Holy See, preventing future intrusions of irresponsible, self-authorized and incompetent reformers.

The Roman Missal of St. Pius V was, then, no new creation or departure from former practice, any more than his Breviary. Rather was it a re-establishing of the Church's most ancient, approved tradition, a getting rid of accretions and innovations, whilst avoiding their replacement by other novelties.[3]

The revised Missal was welcomed, as the Breviary, by the clergy everywhere. Italy, Spain and other

European countries at once adopted it, though again France was slower and it was not, evidently, until a decade later, by means of provincial synods, that some regions began to do so, and the royal household. Some pluralism, not to say anarchy, of rites must have persisted even for quite a while longer in France, and in other countries, else how could St. Vincent de Paul, for one, who was born four years after Pius V died, have referred in his *Conversations* to the ugliness and diversity of former Mass ceremonies, and to having once seen eight priests saying Mass in eight different ways? But there is no record of any widespread distress having been caused to priests or laity by Pius V's revision and legislation of the Roman Missal.

The English martyr-priests, coming into the country from the continent, were of course trained in the Mass promulgated by Pope Pius, from 1570 onwards; and it was the ancient Roman rite, revised and made uniform by Pius V, not any of the other rites then still in existence, that the English people demanded in the uprisings throughout the country against the changes forcibly imposed by Henry,

---

[3] Pius V introduced the psalm *Introibo ad altare Dei* and first *Confiteor* said at the foot of the altar in the old Roman rite. He also inserted the *Suscipe, sancta Trinitas* at the *Lavabo* during the Offertory and regulated the *Hanc Igitur* and *Per Ipsum* of the Canon, as well as the final blessing. The "Last Gospel" from the first chapter of St. John, said voluntarily after the Mass by the priest as part of his thanksgiving since the 13th century, Pius V had included at the end of the Mass, out of devotion to the Incarnation, and to stress the doctrine.

Edward and Elizabeth. None had hitherto complained of the Roman rite, it seems except Wycliffe and the Lollards.

Gregorian plainchant is inseparable from Latin, but in the 16th century it had actually come to be doubted whether any form of sacred music whatever was a fitting accompaniment to divine worship, and its total exclusion from the liturgy was even considered. Palestrina convinced Pope Pius IV that truly noble music can serve true piety by his *Missa Papae Marcelli* composed in honor of the holy Pope Marcellus II who reigned for only three weeks before Pius IV. On the score of Palestrina's masterpiece the words *Help me, O God!* had been written with trembling hand. It remains to be said that Pius V appointed him choirmaster of the papal chapel; and under him Gregorian chant, that had fallen into neglect, was restored to its full beauty and pride of place in the Roman liturgy as the Latin Church's oldest and purest musical expression (reconfirmed by Vatican Council II).

Chapter 7

LAST DAYS AND DEATH

The active life is concerned with men and things; the contemplative is in the realm of supreme truth and has to do with the very principle of life, Almighty God. Christianity's chief business—*officium principalissimum*—St. Thomas Aquinas says, is the union of these two lives: but the contemplative is better than the active: *Vita contemplativa simpliciter melior est. . . et potior quam activa.*[1]

What else but this constant uniting of spiritual contemplation and active works, with preference given to the former, so marvelously maintained by Michael Ghislieri throughout his life as monk, Prior, Bishop, Cardinal and Pontiff, was the source of the radical and far-reaching spiritual and temporal reforms Pius V was able to bring about, in but six years of pontificate, for the Church and Christian civilization? Whether fighting heresy within, or enemies without, dealing with the disloyal Emperor and wayward sovereigns abroad or vice and lawlessness in his own States and Rome, he was all the while by his own self-denial, penances and piety

---

[1] *Summa Theologica*, Pt. II-II, 2.182.

drawing more and more people back to the Faith and practice of true religion.

"In long vigils of silent, interior communion," wrote Evelyn Waugh in his classic biography of St. Edmund Campion, "Pius contemplated only the abiding, abstract principles that lay behind the phantasmagoric changes of human affairs. . . This it was that enabled him to see things and situations with such complete clarity."

From time to time, leaving the Vatican where he lived in a small suite of rooms away from the great state apartments, Pope Pius would take up residence in the Dominican monastery of *Santa Maria sopra Minerva,* or at *Santa Sabina* on the Aventine hill.[2] There, in the still greater silence and peace of the cloister, the Pope whose culminating act in his work of spiritual reform had been to proclaim St. Thomas a Doctor of the Church would live again, sometimes for a few days, as a simple religious, regathering spiritual and physical strength for further enterprise.

During the first year of his reign, he would occasionally pause to go and dine at the papal villa not far from the city,[3] in whose garden, cultivated by

---

[2] The cell in which the Pope slept has been converted into a chapel. There is a painting of St. Pius over the altar by Domenico Muratori. Another painting by Marliani depicts him, when a Cardinal, with St. Philip Neri kneeling at his feet and foretelling that he would be Pope.

[3] This villa still stands today and is situated opposite the cemetery of Calepodius in the Armellini vineyard.

his personal physician with exotic plants and shrub-
bery, he found some rest and refreshment for mind
and body. But later, the sole recreation he allowed
himself was an outing to his beloved *Santa Sabina*.

When Paul IV had made him a Bishop, saying
that he had done so to "chain his feet and prevent
his ever returning to live in monastic seclusion," he
had replied that the Pope was "taking him from
Purgatory to Hell." Now, he told the Venetian ambassador, who noted the conversation, that the trials
and labors of the papacy were far greater causes
of suffering than monastic discipline and poverty,
or any other trial and hardship; and that the dignity of the papal office could come near to being
a hindrance to the soul's salvation.

Never passively resigned to the present course of
events—the "historic moment," as some today like
to call it—he knew no half measures in his dealings. Nothing could make him change his mind once
convinced of what had to be done. But he gave
way on occasion to what he realized was another's
better judgement; nor did he shrink from simply
beginning over again and making due rectification
if by its results a course of action embarked on
proved defective.

Living with the utmost frugality and least possible regard for his own health and comfort, his goodness, humility and generosity towards others went
to heroic lengths. When his nephew Cardinal Bonelli
became seriously ill, Pius looked after him with the
loving care of a parent. But another time, when
he found silk hangings put up in his apartments,

not in keeping with religious poverty, he ordered their removal, refusing to accept the excuse of the major-domo's having done it. Pius' anger grew on learning that his nephew was being counselled by another Cardinal; and he forbade further relations with such severity that it took Cardinal Bonelli some time to recover.

Pius V forgave his enemies, and did good to them. A nobleman who had treated him very badly when Inquisitor, but had forgotten this, was recognized by the Pope during an audience granted to a diplomatic mission. "I am the poor Dominican you once wanted to throw down a well," he quietly said to him. "You see, God protects the weak and innocent." Then quickly putting an end to the man's embarrassment, with one of his rare, enchanting smiles he embraced him and promised special consideration for his mission. A writer, brought before the Pope for libelling him, received no sentence, but was pardoned and told that if in the future he had any fault to find with the Pope he should come and tell him personally about it. Turkish prisoners in Rome acknowledged the kind treatment they had received. Those who had most offended him often became the recipients of his tenderest concern.

He expressed his own readiness for martyrdom, and more than once showed his willingness to die for others. But he said, too, that God, who had called him to the highest office, would at the same time protect him, in spite of what any human power could do.

Characteristic of him was the gratitude he showed in many ways to all who had benefitted him.

Loving and prizing truth above all else, he had a horror of insincerity and feigning.

Such was the holiness of Pius V that his worst foes were often overcome by it. God attested to this great holiness of the Church's head by miracles even during his lifetime. Once, according to several accounts, on stooping to kiss the crucifix before which he was accustomed to meditate in his private apartments, the figure withdrew so that he could not touch it with his lips. The cry of anguish that came from the Pope, who feared he must have done something unworthy to deserve such a rebuke, brought servants running into the room. Hearing what had happened, and the reason for the Pope's distress, they thought differently. Foul play was suspected. The figure was rubbed with bread crumbs and these were given to an animal, which died after eating them. The well-known picture of St. Pius V with the crucifix depicts the pontiff gazing in an attitude of dismay at the withdrawn feet of the figure on the Cross.[4]

The intermittent pains he had long suffered from "stones" at length grew almost unbearable. But he chose to suffer still more rather than be operated

---

[4] This crucifix was kept in the chapel that was once the Pope's cell in the monastery of Santa Sabina, but was removed to the monastery museum for greater safety, together with other precious relics of St. Pius V, including an *Agnus Dei* blessed by him, his spectacles and one of his slippers (the other was stolen).

on and have other people's hands touch his body.

A servant, seeing how weak he had grown in Lent from fasting, tried to get him to take a little more nourishment by surreptitiously adding some meat sauce to his usual diet of wild chicory. Pius, detecting this, reprimanded the man with the words: "My friend, do you wish me during the last few days of my life to break the rule of abstinence I have observed these fifty years?" When he found that the small measure of wine mixed with his water under doctor's orders had been increased, he threatened to dismiss the servant who had done it. His cook was forbidden, under pain of severest sanctions, to put any unlawful ingredients in his soup on days of fasting and abstinence, and during Lent.

Throughout his pontificate, Pope Pius never failed to be present at every prescribed ceremony, even when not feeling well; in addition, though told it was not customary for the Pope to do so, he insisted on attending the funeral rites of all deceased Vatican prelates and clergy.

After the Holy Week ceremonies, on Good Friday, 1572, he was obliged to take to his bed. But ordering the crucifix to be carried into his room, he got up and prostrated himself several times before it.

To his physical pains were added at the last a number of spiritual griefs, mainly caused by the behavior of certain Catholic sovereigns: Philip II's ambassador was threatening rupture of diplomatic relations if the Pope granted a dispensation for Henry of Navarre's marriage which the French ambassador, on the other hand, was seeking to obtain by threatening withdrawal from papal obedience. Pope Pius' disapproval of the marriage at the same time earned him the resentment of Charles IX of France and Catherine de Medici. He could, nevertheless, sing his *Nunc dimittis* in the knowledge that reform of the Church had been achieved in head and members, heresy at least circumscribed and the Turkish peril definitely averted.

It was rumored the Pope was dying.

Informed of the people's sorrow at his illness, and remembering how he had hoped that they would have greater reason to regret his death than some had been disappointed by his election, Pius summoned up all remaining strength to give them his customary Easter Blessing.

A vast crowd gathered in St. Peter's Square, and when the Pope appeared on the balcony of the Basilica, in pontifical vestments, and chanted the Blessing in feeble, but gravely sweet tones, the hush was so intense that his voice could be clearly heard by those farthest off. Many wept for joy, hoping and praying the Pope's life would be prolonged.

Feeling greater strength returning, to the dismay of his physicians, household and Cardinals, Pius then determined to make his regular visit to Rome's seven Basilicas,[5] on foot, and could not be dissuaded. "God who began the work will see it to the end," he said, glancing up at the sky.

---

[5] A custom revived by Pius V and Philip Neri, soon taken up by the Cardinals and court prelates.

At the Lateran, he wanted to climb the Holy Stairs,[6] but was unable to, and kissed the bottom step in tears.

Awaiting him in getting safely back to the Vatican was a group of English Catholics exiled by Elizabeth. The Pope stayed talking to them, and exclaimed before leaving them and recommending them to the care of a Cardinal: "Lord, Thou knowest I have always been ready to shed my blood for their nation."

The day before he died, Pius wished to get up and celebrate Mass for the last time, offering himself in holocaust at the altar. But this he could not do, and had to be satisfied with hearing Mass said in his room.

On the last day of April, aware that his death was approaching, he asked for the Last Sacraments, first rising and going down on his knees, to humble himself before God. He desired to die in his Dominican habit.

After receiving the Viaticum, he addressed his last words to the Cardinals assembled at his bedside. He declared amongst other things that, although his sins and failings had not allowed him to see the final achievement of all he had endeavored to do, he adored God's holy will and accepted His judgments.

---

[6] The 28 steps of Tyrian marble traditionally held to be those of the house of Pilate, and upon which fell drops of the Saviour's blood as He descended them. The stairs were brought to Rome by the Emperor Constantine's mother, St. Helena.

Among his final utterances were repeated incitations to continue the allied crusade against the Turks.

On May 1, in great agony, he lay motionless, except for constant kissing of the crucifix. Those nearest him made out the words, alternated with the prayers he was murmuring: "Lord, increase my pain, but may it please Thee also to increase my patience!"

With this heroic act of love, in utmost peace, and features as never before radiant, Pius V died.

St. Teresa of Avila, who like St. Pius had the gift of prophecy, seems to have been supernaturally aware in that moment of the Pope's passing and told her nuns to mourn as the Church had just lost her most holy Pastor.

On opening his body, the doctors found stones of such size that they wondered how he had been able to live with the pain they must have caused him.

After death, Pope Pius' body remained for some time fresh, supple and fragrant as a child's.

The statue of St. Pius V, in the Sistine Chapel of St. Mary Major's Basilica, Rome, by Leonardo da Sarzana.

Portrait of St. Pius V by Federico Zuccari. (*Reproduced by permission of Stonyhurst College.*)

Chapter 8

MIRACLES, BEATIFICATION AND CANONIZATION, THE MAUSOLEUM IN ST. MARY MAJOR'S BASILICA

In common with many another saint, Pius V had wished for as humble and obscure a place of burial as possible, and at one time he had even made plans to be interred in the Dominican monastery founded by him at his birthplace in North Italy. He thought himself unworthy to be buried in Rome among the tombs of so many holy and renowned predecessors.

But God made use of the gratitude of one of his successors, Sixtus V, [1] toward his life-long friend and benefactor to ensure that the memory of His Servant and Vicar should be perpetrated from the

---

[1] In 1551 the Holy Office Inquisitor General Ghislieri had to question a young and brilliant Franciscan preacher, Felix Peretti, concerning some of the things said in his sermons, after a dramatic denunciation one day in St. Peter's. The candor and loyalty of the priest's replies completely convinced the Inquisitor, who ended by promising him his special protection. When Pope, he favored his election as Minister General of his order, and later made him a Bishop, then Cardinal of Montalto; and Cardinal Montalto it was who succeeded Gregory XIII as Sixtus V.

Eternal City and center of Christianity.

Cardinal Montalto had a chapel built by Fontana on the right side of St. Mary Major's Basilica. On becoming Pope Sixtus V, he would not suffer Pius V's mortal remains, which had lain in the St. Andrew's Chapel of St. Peter's as temporary resting-place, to be removed from Rome. Sixtus had the relics of the Crib,[2] which had previously been brought over from the Holy Land, placed in the new chapel in St. Mary Major's on the site where the popes used to sing the first Christmas Mass before dawn. Here he built a mausoleum for Pope Pius, of white marble from floor to ceiling of the chapel since known as the Sistine. It is now the Chapel of the Blessed Sacrament.

Sixtus V had the cause of Pius V introduced.

In January 1588, Pius V's body was publicly transferred, great crowds assisting, from St. Peter's to St. Mary Major's, where it was laid to rest beneath the monument.

Popular veneration grew steadily until before long, many began privately asking his intercession. More and more miracles were reported. At the process begun in the year 1616, further suffrages were forbidden and it was laid down instead that every year, on the anniversary of Pius V's death, a solemn Mass in honor of the Most Holy Trinity should be celebrated.

A hundred years after his death, at the instance

------

[2] These relics have since been kept in a gold and silver wrought casket under the main altar.

of the King of France and the Master General of the Dominicans, and after two miracles had been chosen for proving,[3] Pius V was beatified by Clement X, in 1672.

Twenty years later, after official recognition, Innocent XII had his remains removed from beneath the monument where they had lain near the little underground chapel containing the relics of the Crib, and placed before the mausoleum in an urn of gilded bronze.

Clement XI canonized Pius V in 1712, in St. Mary Major's Basilica. Miracles attributed to his intercession were by this time so numerous and proven as only to need selection for the two required by the canonization process. Among them were cures of sick persons, deliverance of the possessed, punishment of criminals and innumerable spiritual and physical graces especially through *Agnus Dei* images blessed by him.

One miracle that occurred during his lifetime, frequently recounted, is particularly striking and memorable: the Polish ambassador, speaking with the Pope at the doors of St. Peter's, asked for a relic to take back with him to his country. Pius V stooped, took a little dust from the ground, put this in a piece of clean linen and gave it to the ambassador with the words: "These are very

---

[3] The instant cure of a diseased man by touching a piece of the Pope's habit; and the preservation of two paintings of St. Pius V in a fire that destroyed everything else in the palace of the Duke of Sezze, in which he said his first Mass.

precious relics." Trying not to feel offended, the ambassador had the grace to accept what was offered him. On getting home, he found the linen stained with blood—blood of martyrs that had once watered Roman ground.

In 1824, Pius V's remains were privately redressed in new vestments. But less than a century afterwards, both these remains and the bones had undergone considerable deterioration from the passage of time. In 1904, the Cardinal-Archpriest of St. Mary Major's Basilica, after formal recognition of the skeleton found almost intact, had the bones cleaned for repositioning—this time on silver wire netting for better preservation. It was proposed to leave the skull bare; but as Pius IX had had a metal mask put over it, the bone being much blackened, the idea prevailed of having the saint's features reproduced in silver from the best death mask.

At the repositioning of 1904, the sacred remains were again reclothed in white pontifical vestments. The pectoral cross was given by another Pope, also Pius by name, the only pontiff to have been canonized to date after him.

So the body of Pius V may now be seen each year on the Feast Day, April 30 (formerly May 5), when the front of the urn, with his recumbent effigy in gilded bronze, is opened and an altar set up for Masses to be said over his sacred remains exposed for veneration.

The statue of St. Pius V, seated, crowned and in the act of blessing in the central niche of the mausoleum is by Sarzana. The surrounding bas-reliefs by various artists represent scenes from his pontificate: in the middle, the coronation; on the left, Charles IX's victory over the Huguenots at Moncontour and the mission of Count Santafiora bringing help to France against the Huguenots; on the right, the battle of Lepanto, and Pope Pius receiving the victorious standard from Mark Anthony Colonna. At the foot of the central statue are the words:

> *Pio V Pont. Max.—ex ordine Praedic.*
> *Sixtus V Pont. Max.—ex ord. Minor.—*
> *Grati animi monumentum—Posuit.*

On the other side of the Sistine Chapel of the Blessed Sacrament in St. Mary Major's is the mausoleum, of similar design and dimensions, of Sixtus V.

Until 1965, the flag of a Turkish galley taken during the battle of Lepanto was kept in the chapel sacristy. It was since returned to Istanbul, in an intended friendly token of concord.

> *Flagrans in eo propagandae Religionis Catholicae desiderium: indefessus pro instauranda Ecclesiastica Disciplina labor: incredibilis ac quasi perpetua in extirpandis erroribus vigilantia: ab sublevandam indigentium inopiam prona inexhausta beneficienti pro tuendis Ecclesiae Iuribus ferreum pectus, ac robur invictum.*

These words, extracted from the *Compendium of St. Pius V's Life, Virtues and Miracles* published in 1712 with the Acts of his canonization process, may fittingly bring this brief account to a close.

NOTES

NOTES

NOTES

If you have enjoyed this book, consider making your next selection from among the following . . .

Prices subject to change.

Prices subject to change.

Prices subject to change.

Prices subject to change.

At your Bookdealer or direct from the Publisher.
Toll Free 1-800-437-5876   **Fax 815-226-7770**
Tel. 815-226-7777   **www.tanbooks.com**

Prices subject to change.

Robin Anderson was born in London in 1913. His father, of Scottish ancestry, was a colonel in the Indian Political Service and published stories of British Imperial India; his mother, of Irish origin, was an amateur painter and pianist. Educated at Marlborough College, Anderson studied at the London Royal Academy of Dramatic Art. In 1836 he married the German-Jewish dancer and actress, Valeska Gert, a refugee from Nazi Germany. During the war years, he worked as stage manager for Shakespearean actor John Gielgud. His first short story was published in 1946 in England's top literary magazine, *Horizon*. Converted to Catholicism under the influence of G. M. Hopkins and Cardinal Newman, Anderson in 1953 went to Rome, where he has lived ever since, working as a speaker for Vatican Radio, and teaching languages. Elected a Fellow of the Institute of Linguists in 1961, he has published articles and poetry and lectured on religious and cultural subjects in Italy, England, the United States and other countries. Among his published works are: *The Quiet Grave* (Journals), *Rome Churches for English-speaking People, St. Pius V, Between Two Wars—The Story of Pius XI, Gleams of English-Language Literature,* and *Pope Pius VII.* Collected prose and poems, with Italian and French translations, appeared in 1983. Prof. Anderson is pictured here in the cloisters of St. Paul's-outside-the-walls (Rome, 1985).